LAURENCE MARKS and MAURICE GRAN

THE·NEW STATESMAN

UNEXPURGATED TEXTS

ANDRE DEUTSCH

First published 1992 by
André Deutsch Limited
105-106 Great Russell Street
London WC1B 3LJ

Copyright © 1992 by Yorkshire Television

CIP data for this title is available
from the British Library

ISBN 0 233 98797 5

Printed and bound in Great Britain by
The Hollen Street Press, Slough, Berks

THE·NEW
STATESMAN

CONTENTS

HOUSE OF COMMONS
LONDON SW1A 0AA

The Hon. John Major, MP.PC.MCC
[3 for 27, St Alwyn's Boys Club Brixton,
versus Streatham High School for Girls
Second 11, May 27, 1955]

Dear Johnny,

Here it is, a signed first edition of the first volume
of my memoirs.

You'll see that the cover price is £7.99. However, the
special offer price to you is only £25,000, payable in
small denominations [Nothing larger than a ten pound
note or the Seventh Day Adventists]. Failure to take
advantage of this special offer will lead to the swift
publication of the second volume of my memoirs, dealing
with that memorable fortnight we spent on Robert Maxwell's
yacht.

Lady Thatcher and almost all of the Royal Family have
already agreed to purchase a copy of the book on these
very reasonable terms. If you agree to follow suit, stuff
the bank notes into any large hollow globular vessel
[looking round the cabinet table you'll be spoilt for
choice] and send them via the usual channels to

Your disobedient servant,

Alan B'Stard.

Passport to Freedom

1. INT. HOTEL CORRIDOR. NIGHT.

We hear the lift open and two noisy voices emerge. One belongs to Alan, the other to a young girl, Victoria.

2. INT. HOTEL BEDROOM. NIGHT.

An empty bedroom, typical international Holiday Inn decor. The room is dark. The door opens and in come Alan and Victoria. She is about twenty, quite pretty, Sloane-ish, rather naive, and a House of Commons secretary. Someone turns on the light. Alan and Victoria have had dinner with quite a lot of wine. Their luggage is already in the room. Inside the room they kiss eagerly, though clumsily. They start ripping each other's clothes off. Alan has to take his waistcoat off over his head, because his gold watch chain gets tangled up with the buttons. Still in the process of undressing, they fall onto the bed. Alan turns the light off. After a moment, Victoria turns it on again.

ALAN   Okay we'll do it with the light on!

VICTORIA   I'm sorry, I don't know if I can go through with this.

ALAN *(Gritted teeth)* Well do you mind if I start without you?

VICTORIA I mean I just don't do one-night stands.

ALAN I wish you'd told me before I gave the hotel receptionist my credit card number!

VICTORIA That's a horrible thing to say! *(Moves violently away from him)*

ALAN I'm only joking! *(With excess 'charm')* I'm renowned in Westminster for my sense of humour, my enormous majority . . . *(Moves closer)* and my incredible virility. And Vicky, *(Very sincerely, while leading her back to bed)* this isn't a one-nighter, it's a first-nighter. I love you. I've loved you ever since Brook Street Bureau sent you into my life, yesterday.

VICTORIA Do you really mean that?

ALAN Of course I do. . .

This time Victoria turns off the light. We hear about eight seconds of lustful bonking, with lots of panting and grunting, all from Alan. Then he puts the light on. Alan and Victoria are now under covers, Alan lying back, his hands folded behind his head. He looks smug. She looks confused.

ALAN How was it for you?

VICTORIA   How was what? *(Realises it's all over)* Oh! *(Tries to be tactful)* Well, it was . . . different.

ALAN   In what way different? Sexier? Chunkier? Raunchier?

VICTORIA   Quicker.

ALAN   *(Defensive bravado)* Of course it was quick, I'm a very busy man. I haven't got time to waste! Anyway, I've never understood this obsession with quantity over quality. Orgasm's the objective, isn't it? The magazines my wife reads are full of articles about how to have orgasms! Though why they're printing them in *Farmers' Weekly* is beyond me. Well, I've never had any trouble on the climax front. *(Switches on the TV from the headboard control)* I wonder what's on TV . . . *(Starts channel hopping, from* Newsnight, *to* News at Ten, *to a weird film on Channel Four)* Where's Sergeant Bilko?!

VICTORIA   Alan, did you mean it when you said you loved me?

ALAN   *(Offhand)* 'Course, when I said I loved you, I meant it.

VICTORIA   Only I've never been to bed with a married man before . . . not unless you count Daddy.

ALAN   *(Not paying any attention to her)* Look, shut up will you? This is my favourite commercial. *(Sings along)* 'Say the Leeds and you're smiling. . .'

VICTORIA   I'm so awfully glad you love me, because I forgot to tell you, I'm not on the pill. *(Alan hears this!)* I was on the pill, but I put on two stone and got spots and no one fancied me . . . What would you do if I got pregnant, Alan?

ALAN   *(Glibly)* Leave my wife and marry you, of course. *(Switches off the TV)* In fact I think I'll phone my wife now.

VICTORIA   Alan, darling, you're so impetuous!

ALAN   Oh, be quiet, you stupid typist! *(Picks up the telephone and dials a long distance number. He waits a couple of seconds, then, in a convincing German accent. . .)* Is this Haltemprice Yorkshire, number 35672? I have for you a Herr B'Staadt from Düsseldorf calling.

Intercut between Sarah's bedroom and hotel bedroom

Sarah and Beatrice are in bed, listening to the 'German Operator', coming over the little speaker of a fancy telephone.

ALAN   Hello, fluffy bottom?

Sarah and Beatrice wince in unison.

SARAH   Hello, thumper ... did you have a good flight?

ALAN   Yes, the Germans are terribly efficient ... if you like lashings of sauerkraut for breakfast. We landed ten minutes early, wind assisted flight.

SARAH   You poor bunny. And how's the conference going?

ALAN   It's riveting, if you're interested in Pigmeat Intervention Price Policy for the nineteen nineties. But I do so hate sleeping alone, darling ... *(Runs his hand up Victoria's leg)*

SARAH   So do I, darling . . . *(Beatrice nibbles Sarah's ear. Sarah giggles)*

ALAN   Are you sure you are alone?

SARAH   Oh Alan! As if I could bear to even look at another man! *(Beatrice has to stuff a pillow in her mouth to stop laughing)* What about you?

ALAN   I couldn't sleep with another man either. *(Laughs Alanishly)*

SARAH   I know darling . . . Hurry home . . . *(Beatrice whispers in her ear)* By the way, Beatrice popped in for supper this evening, she said keep it up . . .

ALAN   What?!

SARAH   The good work, darling.

ALAN   Oh, of course. *(Hangs up and jumps on Victoria)*

3. INT. AIRPORT TERMINAL. DAY.

About 10am next day. Inside the busy, noisy airport terminal. There is quite a long queue at the Lufthansa desk. Most of the queuers are Members of Parliament. Piers is quite near the front of the queue. A few places behind him is Bob Crippen, a pugnacious, left-wing Labour MP. Alan hurries through the crowded terminal towards the queue. He sees Piers near the front and goes to stand in front of him, about two places from the check-in desk.

ALAN   Thanks for keeping my place, Piers. Overslept, you know what it's like when you're in the saddle all night boffing some insatiable little sexpot . . . No, you don't know what it's like at all . . .

CRIPPEN   Hey, pal, there's a queue here you know!

ALAN   Don't fret, Crippen, it's an airliner, not a corporation tram, there are seats for everyone! Though heaven knows why you're going to a conference on pigmeat pricing, you represent an inner city slum! Or do your constituents breed pigs on the balconies of their tower blocks?

CRIPPEN   Pigs wouldn't put up with the tower blocks your

miserly Government forces my constituents to live in! And if
we weren't in an airport terminal patrolled by heavily armed
members of the Anti-Terrorist Squad, I'd give you a good
smack for that!

ALAN *(To all and sundry)* You see, there's the voice of the
modern Labour Party. Thinly veiled political thuggery!

CRIPPEN *(Threateningly)* Do you like hospital food?!

ALAN Love it, but then of course I'm in BUPA.

CRIPPEN I'll kill him!!

*Crippen's friends have to restrain him from nutting Alan. Alan
and Piers dodge out of the way.*

ALAN *(To Crippen)* All right, you check in first, if you can't
take a joke.

A glowering Crippen checks in.

PIERS *(It takes Piers a long time to formulate a thought)* Why are *you* coming on this trip, Alan? You're not interested in farming . . .

ALAN I know, but it's all expenses paid, and there are some very naughty clubs in Stuttgart . . .

Having checked in, Crippen stalks away angrily. It is now Alan's turn to check in. He puts his suitcase on the scales. The case goes through onto the conveyor. He gets out his ticket. The Lufthansa girl looks at it.

LUFTHANSA GIRL And your passport please, Herr B'Stard.

Alan goes to get his passport out of his inside jacket pocket, but he can't find it. He looks in other pockets, then starts to worry.

ALAN I'm sure I had it last night . . . *(Piers sniggers)*

LUFTHANSA GIRL There's a long line behind you, would you please stand aside?

ALAN As Hitler said to Chamberlain before he invaded Poland! *(Girl scowls)* Look, my humourless little Valkyrie, I am Alan B'Stard MP, I have the biggest majority in the House of Commons, and I am attending a conference on a subject close to the Germans' soul, namely pigmeat. I don't need a passport, we won the war.

LUFTHANSA GIRL *(Ignoring Alan, to Piers)* If you'd put your luggage on the scales.

PIERS *(Doing so)* Look, Fräulein, I can vouch for him.

LUFTHANSA GIRL Yes, but who will vouch for you?

PIERS Oh . . . *(Thinks)* Alan will vouch for me.

ALAN *(Angry)* I demand to see the manager, or the airport-führer, or whatever you call him!

LUFTHANSA GIRL *(Very annoyed)* I'm afraid Mr Goering is unavailable, he's busy pillaging the art galleries of Eastern Europe.

PIERS Perhaps it's in your attaché case?

ALAN *(Distracted)* What?

PIERS Your passport . . .

ALAN No, I must have left it in Yorkshire. Damn!

PIERS   At least look in your case . . .

ALAN   It is not in my case! *(Starts searching pockets again)*

PIERS   It might be, I'm always losing things and then finding them in unexpected places.

ALAN   That's because you're a congenital idiot.

But Piers picks up Alan's attaché case, puts it on counter, and opens it. It contains Holiday Inn towels, ashtrays, bathmat, electric kettle, hairdryer, etc. Piers, the Lufthansa girl, and other onlookers gaze at Alan, awaiting an explanation.

ALAN   *(With world-weary sophistication)* The lengths these hotels will go to to attract VIP customers.

4. INT. DRAWING ROOM. DAY.

Mid-morning. Sarah, in her silk kimono, and Beatrice, in her business suit, are drinking champagne.

SARAH   . . . Everyone dreams that a long lost relative will die and leave them a fortune, but *(Brandishes a letter)* two hundred thousand shares in Ocelot Motors! I can't believe it!

BEATRICE   *(Referring to her* Financial Times*)* At today's share prices, you're virtually a millionaire!

SARAH   *(Mae West voice)* Virtue has nothing to do with it! *(Own tones)* I was only nine when Uncle Luke retired to South Africa, he was past sixty then! I never imagined he was still alive . . .

BEATRICE   He isn't . . .

SARAH   No, of course not . . . poor Uncle Luke, he was such a sweetie . . . *(Sniffs)*

BEATRICE   *(Drains her champagne)* It couldn't have happened to a nicer person, Sarah . . .

SARAH   I'm sure it could have, but I'm glad it didn't . . . *(As Sarah starts getting her briefcase and handbag)* Where are you going?

BEATRICE   To work, darling. You may now be a very rich lady, but I'm still Alan's agent, on a woeful Conservative Party salary.

SARAH   Don't be silly! There's no need for you to work, now that I'm stinking . . . and anyway, you'll be redundant after I've finished with Alan!

BEATRICE   What do you mean?

SARAH   I can afford to leave him now; a nice messy divorce, with lots of unwelcome publicity for him.

BEATRICE   And that would be the end of his political career!?

SARAH   Exactly.

BEATRICE   Aren't you being a little vindictive, darling?

SARAH   Yes, but he deserves it, now that I know for certain that he cheats on me!

BEATRICE   We cheat on him . . .

SARAH   That's different, we love each other . . . And the world is our oyster, we can do anything, live anywhere, neither of us will ever have to work − not that I ever have . . .

BEATRICE   Sounds fabulous . . . *(Wistfully)* Though I would miss being involved in politics . . .

SARAH   Would you? Then when Alan's forced to resign, you should apply for his seat. I'm sure you'd get it, and then I'd still be the Member's wife.

5. EXT. ALAN'S HOUSE. DAY.

Meanwhile . . . a few hours later. Alan gets out of his Bentley and is busy rehearsing an excuse for Sarah. He repeats it as he walks to his front door.

ALAN   '. . . Then once they found out Piers's AIDS test was positive, they sent us all home!' Yes, that's the one. It's simple . . . like Piers.

6. INT. DRAWING ROOM. DAY.

Sarah, neatly dressed and very composed, is reading a glossy brochure featuring property in the West Indies. Alan's car is heard to pull up outside. She allows herself a half smile. Alan rushes in.

ALAN   I know what you're going to say! What on earth am I doing back in England in the middle of the conference? Well, you're not going to believe this, but we all had routine blood tests last month, and Piers of all people, turns out to be . . .

Sarah stops Alan dead by brandishing his passport.

SARAH   You left this in your bedside drawer.

ALAN   I know. Under the March 1987 Amendment to the European Communtiy Travel Agreement, Members of Parliament on official business don't need . . .

SARAH   Oh shut up, Alan! I'm not Piers! Why don't you just admit you spent last night in an airport hotel with some little typist, for whom I feel nothing but the deepest pity?

ALAN   *(Trying to unnerve her)* I see. Well, if you prefer to think the worst, rather than to listen to my explanation, I just don't know how this marriage is going to survive.

SARAH   It isn't. I've just inherited a million pounds, and I'm going to divorce you.

7. EXT. PARK LANE. DAY.

The next day, Alan gets out of a taxi, and looks around at all the fancy buildings. Then he sees an old Dormobile parked on a corner. It has been wheel-clamped. Alan shrugs, goes to the Dormobile, and raps a coded knock on the back door.

8. INT. DORMOBILE. DAY.

Continuous. The van has been converted into Norman's office for this week, with his familiar office furniture and equipment. Norman is behind his desk. He looks a little more feminine this week, with a touch of blusher on his cheeks. He presses the button that electronically opens the door. Alan enters.

ALAN   *(Sits opposite Norman)* You know you've been wheel-clamped?

NORMAN   Of course. That's the whole object of the exercise.

ALAN   What do you mean?

NORMAN   It's all a matter of perception. You see a clapped-out Dormobile, immobilised by vindictive traffic wardens. I see a hundred square feet of prime office space in Park Lane, fifty pounds a day, and no rates. Now, about your divorce . . .

ALAN   *(Interrupting)* Are you wearing make-up?

NORMAN   Just a hint of blusher . . .

ALAN   It suits you . . . Sorry, go on . . .

NORMAN   Well, as soon as you told me about the divorce, I transferred all your companies to the one country where even the bank accounts of known criminals are safe from official scrutiny.

ALAN   You mean the Vatican City?

NORMAN   Precisely. So your wife won't be able to get her hands on a penny.

ALAN   That's very good, Norman, but the problem isn't *my* money. Sarah's inherited a major stake in Ocelot Motors, that's why she can afford to divorce me!

NORMAN   I see . . . If she's not after your money, it doesn't matter if she leaves you, does it? *(Girlishly)* And if I were your wife . . .

ALAN   Listen, you chartered freak! I'm only MP for Haltemprice because Sarah's father runs the local Conservative party. The second we're divorced, I'll be out on my arse, with about as much chance of finding another seat as a deaf kid in a game of musical chairs!

NORMAN   Oh. It's serious then. I suppose you want me to come up with some ingenious solution?

ALAN   I suppose you want me to continue to pay for your sex change treatment?

NORMAN   Has she actually got the shares in her possession yet?

ALAN   I don't think so, her uncle died abroad, so there are all the legal formalities to go through first . . .

NORMAN   Good, that gives you a little time . . .

ALAN   To do what?

NORMAN   It's obvious . . . Destroy the company, thereby

turning Sarah's shares into waste paper.

ALAN   We're not talking about Joe's Garage! Ocelot is a major sports car producer!

NORMAN   So was De Lorean, and they went bust!

ALAN   Ocelot aren't De Lorean! Ocelot make proper cars!

NORMAN   So stop them.

9. INT. ALAN'S OFFICE. NIGHT.

That night, Alan is in his office, on the phone, glass of brandy in hand.

ALAN   . . . Have a very hot bath and drink a bottle of gin, and if that doesn't work, call me tomorrow. . . . No, of course I don't love you, grow up, Victoria! *(Hangs up, finishes his drink. Piers*

enters at this point, carrying a pile of photocopies and other documents) Where have you been!? I sent you to the library hours ago, I hope you haven't been wasting your time voting!

PIERS   The photocopying machine broke down, I had to wait for the man . . .

ALAN   Then you should have copied them out by hand! Come on, give . . . ! *(Takes papers from Piers)*

PIERS   *(With a small display of spirit)* I'm not your servant, Alan!

ALAN   If you were I'd have sacked you long ago. *(Unlocks deep desk drawer to reveal large stock of booze, and pours himself another brandy)*

PIERS   Er . . . do you think I could have a drink?

ALAN   *(Locking up his drinks drawer)* I don't see why not; just make sure you're back from the bar by eleven, I might need you . . . *(Alan sits at his desk, a disappointed Piers stays put)* Right, company report, 1986-7 . . . *(Starts to read aloud)* 'Profits up 34% . . . dividends up 42% . . . exports up 61% . . . workforce up by 3,500 . . .'

PIERS   Makes you proud to be British, doesn't it?

ALAN   Shut up, Piers! . . . 'No-strike agreement extended for further five years. . .' It would be easier to bankrupt Paul McCartney! *(Throws report down)*

PIERS   *(Engrossed in a glossy car magazine)* Listen to this! 'The latest Ocelot 3.8 Turbo Supercat, built at their new two hundred million pound factory in Bramall, is a world beater. My test model sleekly muscled its way from nought to sixty in seven and a half seconds . . .' Wish I had one!

ALAN   What are you droning on about?!

PIERS   It's not me, it's Anneka Rice, writing in this month's issue of *Yuppie Car*. I wish I was a Yuppie . . . What does Yuppie actually mean?

ALAN   Yuppie is short for 'Useless Pill', so you are one, congratulations.

PIERS   If I'm so useless, why do you always get me to run all of your errands?

ALAN   Don't be cheeky, Piers, there's a river outside the window, and you can't swim.

PIERS   I can!

ALAN   Not if I tie your hands and feet together . . . *(Suddenly something that Piers read out clicks in Alan's mind)* Piers, where did you say Ocelot had their new factory?

PIERS   *(Childishly)* I'm not telling you. *(Alan raises his hand to Piers, who flinches)* A place called Bramall . . .

ALAN   Bramall!? That's Crippen's constituency! Piers, you're a genius! Come on, we're going to break into the Prime Minister's office!

PIERS   Oh, no! I draw the line there, Alan. I know I let you talk me into all sorts of things because I'm frightened of you, but I'm more frightened of Her!

ALAN   If you help me, I'll get you one of those Ocelot Supercats.

PIERS   Really? Do you promise?

ALAN   No, but I promise that if you don't help me, I won't get you an Ocelot Supercat. . .

10. INT. CORRIDOR. NIGHT.

A little while later, Alan and Piers are walking along an empty corridor somewhere in the Palace of Westminster. Alan is trying to look nonchalant, Piers is looking furtive.

ALAN   Piers, will you stop tip-toeing along like Wee Willie Winkie!? We're not trespassing . . .

PIERS   Yet . . .

ALAN   Look, it's perfectly safe, she's flown to Washington for the unveiling of President Reagan's new nose.

PIERS   Suppose we bump into someone else . . . ?!

ALAN   At this time of night?

Piers and Alan turn a corner, and find a police constable standing around on security duty. He wears a side arm. Quick thinking is called for from Alan. The copper's name is Austin.

AUSTIN   And where do you think you gentlemen are going?

ALAN   It's quite all right, Constable, we're just taking a stroll, drinking in the historic ambience . . .

AUSTIN   I'll have to ask you to identify yourselves, sir, several
ministerial offices on this floor, can't be too careful . . .

ALAN   I quite understand . . . *(Produces some ID)*

AUSTIN   *(Reacts to Alan's name on ID)* You're Alan Bastard!?

ALAN   *(Stressing the correct pronunciation)* B'Stard . . .

AUSTIN   You're the Member who got that Bill through arming
us police, aren't you?!

ALAN   Indeed, I'm proud to say that was I. It wasn't easy, but I
felt you chaps deserved the tools to do the job.

AUSTIN   Oh, I'm a big fan of yours, sir. If I shook you by the
hand, would it be a terrible liberty?

ALAN   Yes it would . . . but just this once . . . *(Allows hand to be
shaken)* This is Piers Fletcher Dervish, who helped draft the
Bill, probably the sharpest legal brain in this corridor at the
moment.

AUSTIN   *(To Piers)* It's a real honour, sir . . .

PIERS   *(Surprised)* Is it!?

ALAN   Tell me, Constable, do you find the gun makes a great deal of difference to your work?

AUSTIN   A revelation, sir. Take Saturday. I'm on detached duty at the Chelsea match; some hooligan throws a bottle onto the pitch, so I draw my piece and blow him all over the half-time scoreboard, splat!

PIERS   Eugh!!

AUSTIN   Wasn't no trouble after that sir. Yes, you've done us Bobbies a right favour. I mean, in this day and age, what good's a truncheon? . . . Though the wife likes it, mind, when I'm on nights. Something for her to grab hold of if she thinks she hears an intruder . . .

ALAN   Constable, since we're such kindred spirits, I wonder if you could do us a small favour?

AUSTIN   If I can, sir.

ALAN   Actually, it's Mr Fletcher Dervish here, he's never been in a minister's room, and unlike me he's never likely to get the opportunity. Could you let him have a peek in one of the offices? Needn't be anything grand, Agriculture, Fish and Food, Northern Ireland even . . .

AUSTIN   Well . . . I don't know, sir, shouldn't leave my post . . .

ALAN   I'll keep an eye out for you . . .

AUSTIN   All right, Mr B'Stard, as it's you . . . *(Takes Piers off down the corridor)* This here's the office of the Chancellor of the Duchy of Lancaster, whatever that is. *(He ushers Piers through into a minister's room and closes door behind them)*

Alan swiftly crosses to another door, which bears the plate − 'Prime Minister's Office'. Alan tries the handle of the door. The door opens.

11. INT. PM's OUTER OFFICE. NIGHT.

Continuous. Alan enters the small ante-chamber to the PM's office. It contains a receptionist's desk, and other office stuff. Alan crosses to the interior door that leads to the inner sanctum, but this is securely locked. He is not surprised. He turns his attention to the desk. The drawers are locked. He takes his Swiss army knife out and springs the lock on the top drawer. It contains stationery bearing the PM's crest. He purloins some sheets and relocks the drawer.

12. EXT. BRAMALL. DAY.

A wide shot of Bramall. It is an industrial town, rather like Halifax. Lots of smoke and chimneys etc.

13. EXT. OCELOT FACTORY. DAY.

Piers, looking furtive in dark glasses, walks into shot, in front of ultra-modern Ocelot factory. Opposite the factory gates is a pillar box. Piers posts a letter, turns and retraces his steps.

14. INT. COMMONS CHAMBER. DAY.

A couple of days later. The House is in uproar. Bob Crippen is on his feet making an angry speech. Alan relaxes in his seat, smiling to himself. Next to him sits Piers, keeping his face blank.

CRIPPEN . . . I don't care how many times the Minister denies it, I've got it here in black and white, on the Prime Minister's own notepaper! *(Reads)* 'My Government fully supports the proposal of the Board of Ocelot Motors to de-unionise their factories and reduce wages by thirty per cent, to ensure price competitiveness into the next decade'!

MINISTER *(Standing)* I don't know where the Honourable Member for Bramall obtained this ludicrous mis-information . . .

CRIPPEN And I'm not bloody telling you, pal!!

SPEAKER Order, order!!

ALAN *(S/V to Piers)* I think it's all going rather well, don't you?

PIERS Do I get a choice of colours?

ALAN What?

PIERS I fancy a black one ...

ALAN What!?

PIERS My new Ocelot Supercat.

CRIPPEN ... But some public spirited employee of Ocelot has had the decency to leak this letter to me, and I will not betray his solidarity! For I myself am a member of the National Union of Car Workers, and I share the Ocelot workers' anger at this betrayal! We signed no-strike agreements with Ocelot, and they turn round and kick us in the ball bearings! *(Alan stands)* I will briefly yield to the Honourable Member for Haltemprice, because it's always enlightening to listen to the crypto-fascist ravings of the loony right! Though I doubt if even he can find a way to justify this scandalous conspiracy!

ALAN Au contraire, Mr Speaker, which I translate as 'That's what you think!' for the benefit of the Member for Bramall, who probably never went to school! *(Tory cheers)* I'm sure all of us on this side of the House are sick and tired of this typical lefty Trot whingeing! It's a hard competitive world out there, and if British products are to hold their own with cheap, Third World goods, we will have to adopt cheap, Third World practices! A car worker in Korea earns fifty pounds a week. A car worker in Bramall earns two hundred pounds a week! Utter folly! It's not as if the average car worker has the taste and intelligence to spend the money on anything more worthwhile than pigeons, whippets, brown ale and oven ready chips! *(Crippen stands, fuming)* I have a personal stake in Ocelot Motors. My wife is a major shareholder. Yet if Mr Crippen's moronic minions choose to embark on a lengthy and crippling strike, destroying the company and rendering its shares worthless, I still say the management should stand firm for the sake of the next generation!

PIERS *(When kicked by Alan)* Hear hear!!

MINISTER I can only repeat that no one in this Government ... *(Drowned by the uproar)*

SPEAKER Order! Order! Order!

15. EXT. OCELOT FACTORY. NIGHT.

Five weeks later, outside the Ocelot factory in Bramall. The gates are barred, and about a dozen men picket. There are banners draped over the gate, and a van for the strikers to brew up in. There's a brazier for them to warm their hands at. The strikers seem rather dispirited.

STRIKER 1   Happen the management was telling truth . . . ?

STRIKER 2   The letter were on't Prime Minister's own bloody writing paper . . . !

STRIKER 1   Well, all I know is t'building society's making threatening noises, and we've had to cancel our skiing holiday . . .

Another man joins in at this point. He is Alan, though the strikers (and audience) don't know this, as he wears a donkey jacket and a balaclava helmet.

ALAN   *(Yorkshire accent)* Bloody skiing holiday?! You're a disgrace to t'memory of Tolpuddle Martyrs! We've been out five weeks now, another few months and the management'll cave in, you mark my words! But go back, and we'll be on coolie wages for t'rest of our working lives! Now cheer bloody up, and who's for a fish supper, on me? *(The other strikers raise their hands)* Right, I'll not be long. *(Strides off)*

STRIKER 2 *(Watching Alan turn a corner)* Who was that masked man?

16. EXT. BRAMALL STREET. NIGHT.

Alan hurries up a side street, to his Bentley. Unlocks door and gets in.

17. INT. BENTLEY. NIGHT.

Alan removes balaclava, allowing audience to identify him, and drives off, grinning.

18. INT. DRAWING ROOM. NIGHT.

A couple of hours later, Sarah is angrily ripping up brochures of exotic holidays and homes, and dropping the pages into a waste bin. Alan enters, crosses to drinks cabinet and pours himself a large brandy.

ALAN Can I get you a drink, darling? *(No reaction from Sarah)* Some warm olive oil to syringe your ears?

SARAH *(Angrily)* I heard what you said!

ALAN Good, in that case, tell me, are you still going through with the divorce?

SARAH How can I, now that my Ocelot shares have been devalued by ninety-seven per cent by a vicious strike that coincidentally started immediately after you found out I was going to leave you?!

ALAN Sarah, surely you can't believe an ordinary backbencher could foment a major strike to save his marriage?!

SARAH   You're not an ordinary backbencher.

ALAN   True, and I admit I do love you enough to do anything in my power to stop you divorcing me . . .

SARAH   You don't love me! You don't love anyone except yourself! All you want is to keep your rotten seat in Parliament, that's what you need me for!

ALAN   Sarah, darling, why so bitter? I admit I made a silly mistake with a secretary! She was a temp, and I was tempted. I'm only human. But that's history now. Let's put it behind us, and go forward together to a brighter tomorrow.

SARAH   You don't know the difference between a declaration of love and a Party political broadcast! All right, you've won, I'm not divorcing you; but that doesn't mean I want to have anything to do with you ever again!

ALAN   But that's not good enough, Sarah. A politician, especially a Tory politician, needs his wife at his side at key moments in his career. It's not a lot to ask. If Joan Kennedy was prepared to help Teddy run for President when they hadn't spoken for five years, I'm bloody sure you can stand next to me at the odd constituency do . . .

SARAH   Give me one reason!

ALAN   I'll double your allowance . . .

SARAH   *(Deciding this is the moment to give in gracefully)* I suppose I ought to give you another chance, marriage should be worked at, after all.

ALAN   I know, and I'll try to come home more at weekends so we can spend those precious days together.

SARAH   I'd rather you didn't, Alan, just remember the allowance . . . and I don't know whether I've told you this, but I've always rather fancied a yacht . . .

19. INT. ALAN'S OFFICE. DAY.

A couple of days later, Alan is in the office, chatting to a pretty new secretary.

ALAN   . . . Yes, our last secretary left to have a baby . . . So, I suppose you'll be getting married soon, pretty girl like you?

PIERS *(Entering)* Am I interrupting, Alan?

ALAN Not this time, Piers . . . *(To secretary)* See you tonight then . . . ? *(Ushers her out)*

PIERS Seen the *Financial Times* today?

ALAN No, why?

PIERS Stock Exchange has suspended dealing in Ocelot shares, so I don't suppose Sarah will be divorcing you now . . . ?

ALAN So?

PIERS You said you'd get me a black Ocelot Supercat if I helped you . . .

ALAN Did you really believe me?

PIERS *(Looks crestfallen)* Did at the time. I suppose I'm just really very stupid . . .

ALAN Yes you are, Piers. Stupid – but loyal. Follow me. *(Exits office)*

20. EXT. COMMONS CAR PARK. DAY.

Alan and Piers enter an underground car park, which is full of expensive cars. One of them is a beautiful, gleaming black 'Supercat' (YTV can either design and build this car from scratch for about seventy-five million pounds, or cosmetically alter something like a TVR or an AC Cobra)

ALAN There she is. *(Hands Piers the keys)*

PIERS *(Gobstruck)* It's beautiful. Thank you, Alan . . .

ALAN My pleasure . . . *(As Piers runs a loving hand over the paintwork)* I gave Hertz your credit card number, you can settle up with them when you take it back. It's eighty-five pounds a day, or four hundred pounds for the week . . .

PIERS You're a bastard, Alan!

ALAN B'stard, Piers.

'The Friends of
St James'

1. EXT. PUBLIC SCHOOL. DAY.

Under the opening music we see Fiskes, a noble English public school, albeit of the minor variety. A rambling Victorian pile in extensive grounds. We see cars, most of them rather expensive, bringing proud parents to the annual Founders' Day prize giving. Alan's Bentley drives in and parks in a reserved space. He gets out. In opening his car door, Alan makes a nasty dent in the wing of a new Montego parked alongside. Alan checks his own car for damage, and is pleased to see there is none. Without even looking at the scarred Montego, he turns and walks towards the main entrance of the school. Many other visitors — well-heeled parents, and some old boys — are also going towards the school buildings. In the background, a well-scrubbed ten-year-old boy runs up to a rather unpleasant nouveau riche couple in their thirties who are getting out of their Range Rover. We close up on ...

BOY Hello, super of you to come ...

MAN *(Brusquely)* We had to, our son's a pupil here. Costs a fortune, but at least it keeps him out of our hair ...

WOMAN *(S/V to man)* Roderick, this is our son!

MAN   *(Looks closely at child)* So it is! Roddy, how you've grown!

2. INT. HEAD'S STUDY. DAY.

The headmaster, a man nearing sixty, is hosting a little sherry reception pre-prize giving. Present are Alan, some other guests, and senior teachers. All have sherry glasses in hand. A white-jacketed waiter, very old, slowly circulates, refilling glasses. Alan is part of a group listening to a fat middle-aged businessman holding forth.

BUSINESSMAN   ... And in five years I'd built my turnover up to thirty million per annum ...

ALAN   *(Impressed)* Thirty million?! Ever thought of having an MP on your letterhead? Good for the old corporate image ...

BUSINESSMAN   Then I said to myself 'What's it all for? Is it making you happy?'

ALAN   It would make me happy.

BUSINESSMAN   So I gave the company away to the workers and went to live in Nepal.

ALAN   Gave it to the workers? That's treason!

BUSINESSMAN   In Kathmandu, I studied under the great Lama ...

But Alan, having lost interest in the businessman, wanders off, looking for someone more useful to talk to. Meanwhile, Lance Okum-Martin, a handsome West Indian old Fiskean of about twenty-seven, has been waiting for a chance to buttonhole Alan. Lance wears a smart navy and red military uniform. He sneaks up on Alan's blind side.

LANCE   Alan, long time no see!

ALAN   *(Spins to confront Lance)* Do I know you?

LANCE   Lance Okum-Martin! I used to be your fag!

ALAN   *(Penny drops)* Of course, Little Lance! So what's become of you since school? No, don't tell me, let me guess. *(Looks him down and up)* Doorman at the Empire, Leicester Square? *(Flicks Lance's epaulettes)* No, must be at least Senior

Doorman, with all this braid! Well done Lance! I'll look you up if I'm ever in the market for two front stalls. *(Moves away)*

LANCE   *(Puts a restraining hand on Alan's arm)* Actually, old boy, the uniform denotes that I'm President for Life of The Republic of St James.

ALAN   *(Interested now)* Really! President for Life? Must pay well . . .

LANCE   It's only a very small, very poor island, Alan.

ALAN   *(Doesn't believe him)* Of course, of course, all you Third World countries are stony broke, but that doesn't seem to stop you Presidents for Life all running seventeen wives and a fleet of Mercedes.

LANCE   Not me, old boy. One fiancée and a Sinclair C5.

ALAN   Pull the other leg, it's got a handmade shoe on . . .

LANCE   Truly. We are poor because we don't have any banks, so it's very hard for our farmers to obtain finance for their unique tobacco exports.

ALAN   *(Losing interest)* Yes, well, it's been marvellous seeing you again, we must do this every twelve years.

LANCE   Can't you help us, Alan, as a Member of Parliament, and for the sake of the old school?

ALAN   No. *(Stops ancient waiter as he passes)* I wonder if, as a Guest of Honour, I'm entitled to a second schooner of Cypriot Amontillado? *(Waiter refills Alan's glass with trembling hands)*

LANCE   *(Insistently)* But our St James's tobacco is very special. At least try some. *(He produces a gold cigarette case which contains neat cheroots. Alan shrugs and takes one. Lance lights it with his gold lighter. Lance waits while Alan takes a few puffs. The effect is almost instantaneous)* Mellow, wouldn't you say?

ALAN   Yes, it's certainly . . . *(Inhales again)* certainly, certainly . . . *(Tails off, rocking slightly on his heels)*

LANCE   *(Urgently)* I don't suppose you could lend me a hundred pounds? Only, coming from a country without any banks . . .

ALAN   Certainly . . . certainly . . . *(Takes out his wallet)* Certainly.

3. INT. SCHOOL HALL. DAY.

Half an hour later. The hall is full of pupils, parents, and old boys. The headmaster is finishing his introductory speech. Alan sits with other guests and staff on the stage, giggling, and trying to hide the fact. Lance Okum-Martin sits next to him.

HEADMASTER ... So with no more ado, I call upon the Member of Parliament for Haltemprice, Yorkshire; Old Fiskean, and future Prime Minister, *(Alan tries to supress a laugh and it comes out a raspberry)* Alan Beresford B'Stard.

Alan gets unsteadily to his feet and goes to the lectern, which he grips until the room stops going around.

ALAN Thank you Headmaster ... With no more ado ... what is an ado? I mean, I've never had one, so how can I have more? *(Giggles)* Just a thought. *(A little sycophantic laughter from audience. Alan gets a page of notes out of pocket)* Clear thinking, and straight talking, that's what I stand for . . . *(Looks at blank page)* Where have my notes gone? *(Turns page over)* Oh, they're written on the other side. Excellent. Okay . . . right . . . Now, why've I got the bigget majority in the House of Commons? . . . Anyone? I'll tell you; it's because more people voted for me than anyone else, of course! They all put their crosses in my box. Pathetic, the number of people who can't even write their names! And if it wasn't for the football pools they

wouldn't even be able to scrawl a cross! That's why we need schools like this one, to keep us apart from them, to stop us being dragged down. So don't talk to me about the education crisis. Look around this beautiful school. Nothing wrong with the education system that two thousand five hundred pounds a term can't put right, is there? *(Members of audience nod)*

Ditto the so-called housing shortage. There are thousands of empty houses if you know where to look. I mean, the Algarve is empty six months out of the year. Yes, what we need in this country are radical solutions, shooting straight from the hip, which brings us on to the Health Service. Now, what to do about waiting lists? Answer's obvious: shut down the Health Service, no more lists. After all, in the good old days, you got ill, and if you were poor, you died. Today, everyone seems to think they have the right to be cured. Result of this sloppy socialist thinking? More poor people. So much for progress. And likewise the unemployment problem. Do away with the dole, no point people signing on, so no more unemployment. No more unemployment, no more so-called north-south divide. Not that there ever was such a thing, everyone knows there are hundreds of millionaires in Scotland . . . least there are during the grouse-shooting season. I could do justice to a brace of grouse now . . . or a bar of chocolate. Thank you very much.

Alan returns to his seat. There is a stunned silence, then a tumultuous standing ovation.

4. INT. CHURCH. DAY.

This week, Norman Bormann has his office set up inside an old church. He is still essentially a man. His suit has seen better days, like Norman. He has several newspapers on the desk. There is an entryphone-type buzz. Norman presses a button on the complicated telephone and speaks.

NORMAN Yes?

ALAN *(Heard on loudspeaker on Norman's desk, with voice disguised)* Inspector McKenzie, Inland Revenue Investigation Department.

Norman leaps up, starts emptying the contents of his desk into his litter bin. Alan still posing as Inspector McKenzie. He speaks into entryphone.

ALAN Come on Bormann, we know you're in there! The

game's up, we know all about your part in the Chernobyl time share scandal ...

Inside the church. Norman speaks into intercom.

NORMAN   This is the Reverend DuBarry, I have no idea what you are talking about! *(Finds his cigarette lighter and is about to ignite the bin)*

ALAN   *(O.O.V. normal voice)* Norman, before you set fire to your litter bin, it's only me being funny ...

Norman pauses with the flaming lighter inches from the bin, but keeps his guard up.

NORMAN   Evensong is at six thirty. We have to keep the church locked up because of the vandals and the tourists.

ALAN   *(O.O.V. long suffering, gives the password)* Edwina Currie likes it hot and spicy.

NORMAN   Does she really?!

ALAN   *(O.O.V.)* That's the password, isn't it?

NORMAN   Oh, yes, of course ... *(Relieved, he lets his cigarette lighter go out, and presses a button on his desk. The church door opens, and bright daylight silhouettes Alan. He enters and crosses to Norman)*

NORMAN   I wish you wouldn't do things like that, Alan. You know the hormone treatment plays havoc with my blood pressure ... You weren't followed, were you?

ALAN   No, of course not ... How is the sex-change going, anyway?

NORMAN   It's a slow process ... *(Hands Alan The Daily Telegraph)* Your speech went down well, the *Telegraph*'s talking about you as a future PM.

ALAN   *(Takes paper from Norman, glances at it)* Only page seven though ... Mind if I take a pew?

NORMAN   Take them all, it's not my church.

ALAN   *(Sits)* Norman, what do you know about St James?

NORMAN   Do you mean St James the Great, son of the fisherman Zebedee, St James the Just, eldest of the brethren of Jesus, or St James the Park, home of Newcastle United football club?

ALAN I don't mean any of those, you encyclopaedic noodle! I
refer to St James the island ...

NORMAN Doesn't ring any tills. *(Takes his* Whitaker's Alma-
nac *out of desk drawer and riffs through the index)* Ah, here it is.
(Reads) 'St James, Caribbean island ... Thirty seven square
miles ... Capital, St James City ...'

ALAN An original mind at work there ...

NORMAN 'Population nine thousand, two hundred ... President for Life, The Honourable L.F.K. Okum-Martin ...'
What about it?

ALAN I met Okum-Martin yesterday at my old school founders' day. Used to be my fag.

NORMAN They allowed black boys in your school?!

ALAN Of course. It was a very liberal regime, as long as they
could afford the fees and didn't mind being called velcro-
bonce. Anyway, I lent him a hundred pounds...

NORMAN And you made him put his island up as security?

ALAN Why didn't I think of that?!

NORMAN But why should the President of a sovereign nation
state be short of the necessary?

ALAN It's a very small island and they don't have any banks,
apparently.

NORMAN No banks!? *(Gets up and starts pacing the aisle)* How
very interesting.

ALAN Interesting? I was rigid with boredom. Explain.

NORMAN If there aren't any banks, then you ought to get him
to let you start one. We could make millions!

ALAN Millions? That's my favourite number! How?

NORMAN We offer high interest rates, no taxation, no exchange controls, and total confidentiality. Then when you've
ensnared a sufficient number of avaricious cretins ...

ALAN Prudent investors ...

NORMAN To deposit their ill-gotten gains ...

ALAN Hard earned savings ...

NORMAN Well, then ... *(Pauses for effect)*

ALAN *(Impatiently)* Yes, yes?!

NORMAN The bank goes out of business and all the money
disappears.

ALAN Into my pocket? *(Norman nods)* Brilliant, let's do it! *(Pause)* What's the catch?

NORMAN You'll have to find a large number of rather stupid and very greedy people with enough money to invest in a dubious get-rich-quick scheme like this.

ALAN Piece of gateau. I mean, where do I work, Norman?

5. INT. COMMONS STRANGERS' BAR. NIGHT.

Alan is having a drink with Lance Okum-Martin, who wears a very smart, conservative business suit. Lance is nervous, but hides it well. As we open, a waiter has just brought their drinks.

ALAN I suppose you're wondering why I invited you here tonight, Lance?

LANCE Alan, if you're worried about your hundred pounds, I'm expecting an international letter of credit from the World Health Organisation for fifty thousand pounds. It's supposed to be for a new clinic, but as I'm also Minister of Health . . .

ALAN Don't worry about the money . . . Cheers! *(Raises glass)*

LANCE *(Pleased at Alan's generosity)* Bottoms up.

ALAN As we used to say in the fifth form remove . . . You see, I want you to consider the hundred pounds as an investment in your poor but worthy homeland.

LANCE What do you mean, exactly?

ALAN I've been worrying about the sorry plight of your struggling, impoverished little farmers, and I think I might be able to help; so I'm prepared to set up a bank for you.

LANCE *(Feeling things are getting out of control)* Oh, that's very considerate, but there's really no need. We're a simple people . . .

ALAN No, no, no, it's the least I can do for an Old Fiskean. All I need is your go-ahead . . .

LANCE *(Still trying to extricate himself)* Well, constitutionally speaking, I should consult the National Representative Council . . .

ALAN Oh come off it, Lance! You're President for Life, don't go pretending it's a democracy! *(Gets some papers out of case)* My advisors have drawn up the relevant documents, all we need is your signature on these papers. *(Produces several imposing documents)*

LANCE *(Thinking, 'In for a penny . . .')* If you're absolutely sure . . . But I think there should be something rather more in it for me than your admittedly gracious hundred pounds.

ALAN Of course, and there is. As President for Life, we would be honoured to have you on our board of directors, and so you'd get the usual kickbacks . . . I mean, dividends.

LANCE That's only to be expected. But tell me, Alan, where do you propose to house this bank? After all, office accommodation is in very short supply on our tiny, overcrowded island.

ALAN I see . . .

LANCE Happily, as Minister of Commercial Development, I own the only office building . . .

ALAN *(Reaching for wallet)* How much?

6. INT. COMMONS CHAMBER. NIGHT.

Thursday night, a week later, about 11pm. The chamber is nearly empty, as most Members have long since left the house for their clubs, or their beds. In progress is an adjournment debate on foreign aid. Alan is in attendance (uncharacteristically), as are about twenty-five other Members and one dozing minister asleep on the front bench. (There has to be at least one minister present, but he doesn't have to be awake). As we open, Catchpole, a Labour shadow minister, is making a boring speech.

CATCHPOLE *(Brummy accent)* . . . But this country dedicates a smaller percentage of its gross national product to multilateral foreign aid than any other member of the European Community. I have the figures here; United Kingdom: 0.47%, Federal Republic of Germany 0.85% . . .

We hear the ringing of a portable Cellnet telephone. Alan removes handset from pocket and extends the aerial.

ALAN   *(Into phone)* Yes? No, it shouldn't go on much longer . . . Because I'm going to speak! Yes, I've got the olive oil . . . Have you got the block and tackle? . . . Great! Now just remind me, it's second left off Streatham High Road, isn't it . . . ?

CATCHPOLE   *(Continuing in the background)* . . . France 0.66%, Luxembourg 1.25% . . . *(Alan stands here, having finished his phone call)* No, I do not give way to the Honourable Member for Haltemprice, I've got a lot more statistics to give the House . . .

ALAN   The House doesn't want them! The House needs your statistics like it needs another Guy Fawkes!

CATCHPOLE   . . . Italy 0.75%, Holland 0.89%, Denmark 0.77% . . .

ALAN   Oh, shut up! This is even more mind-numbing than the Eurovision Song Contest . . .

CATCHPOLE   France . . .

ALAN   You said France! Caught you, sit down!

SPEAKER   Order, order . . .

CATCHPOLE   *(Trying to be funny)* If I said France twice, it's because it's a very important country.

ALAN   Ha, ha, ha, that was meant to be a joke, wasn't it? Only I don't see Mr Speaker laughing, and we all know he has a sense of humour, look at the way he's dressed. *(Catchpole sits, defeated. Alan adopts a Parliamentary pose)* We have heard the Honourable Member for Birmingham Stetchford, a depressingly dreary little constituency which he suits admirably . . . *(Angry noises from Catchpole)* . . . droning on and on in soporific detail, about how we don't give enough foreign aid! I say we give too much, particularly to tinpot little dictators who aren't even decently grateful! If we must give our money away to foreigners, we should give it to pro-British tinpot dictators! *(There are a few automatic 'hear hears' from somnolent old Tories, and cries of 'rubbish' from the opposition)* We should aid our allies, such as the loyal little nation of St James. This brave country, which offered its services to Great Britain during the Falklands conflict. *(A Labour member shouts 'Maggie's election stunt'!)* They were willing – nay, eager – to be used as a strategic staging post. That they proved to be in the wrong ocean wasn't their fault, but a cruel trick of geography. And yet what aid do these fine people receive? Not a farthing! Yet here is a struggling little country that has not taken the communist path; that indeed is so keen to encourage foreign investment that the Bank of St James pays twenty-five per cent tax free interest on foreign deposits of over one hundred thousand pounds . . . That's right. *(Louder)* Twenty-five per cent tax free! *(The whole chamber wakes up at this, and there is a general hubbub, in which the phrase 'twenty-five per cent' is repeatedly heard. Then Alan's Cellnet phone rings. Alan hisses into mouthpiece)* Not now! *(and turns phone off)*

CATCHPOLE *(Standing)* Twenty-five per cent tax free!! Any likelihood of them opening a branch in my constituency?

ALAN Even trees don't have branches in your constituency!

7. INT. CORRIDOR. DAY.

Following Tuesday. A corridor in the Palace of Westminster, lined with committee room doors. On one door a sign says 'Parliamentary Friends of St James, Inaugural Meeting, 3pm'. A good number of Members are filing in. A lot of them are obviously Tories, by their business suits. But there is also a smattering of sports jacketed, wispy-bearded socialists with their collars turned up. Several members are still trying to get in when Alan happily comes out and sticks a 'House Full' sign on the door.

8. INT. COMMITTEE ROOM. DAY.

Fifteen minutes later, inside a packed committee room. At one end, a long table, behind which sits Alan. On an easel behind him is a huge map of the Caribbean, with a big arrow pointing to a tiny dot. The arrow is marked 'St James'. In the front row of the 'audience' sits Piers Fletcher Dervish. Most of the people in the room (but neither Alan nor Piers) are smoking St James cheroots — with significant effects on their personalities. A pall of smoke hangs over the room. Each prospective 'friend' of St James has been equipped with a glossy folder extolling the island and its banking system.

ALAN   ... And I'm sure you'll all agree that this marvellous tobacco deserves the financial backing to compete on the international market. *(Notices Catchpole is giggling helplessly at the back of the room)* The Shadow Spokesman for Foreign Affairs can either stop his childish giggling or go and stand in the corridor.

CATCHPOLE   I'm sorry, I just can't help it . . . *(Sets off several others)*

Another MP, Fiddick, puts up his hand, in which he holds an unlit cheroot.

FIDDICK   Mr Chairman, are you absolutely sure this is tobacco? *(Sniffs the air accusingly)*

ALAN   Are you absolutely sure you're a whining little cheesemite? This is the real world, nothing is sure! Go and live in Albania if it's certainty you want! *(Fiddick sits, squashed)* Now, with the parliamentary recess approaching, I propose that we, The Friends of St James, fly out to this beleaguered little island to study its problems at first hand.

Alan winks at Piers, who takes a second to get the cue, but then stands.

PIERS   *(Parrot fashion)* I second the proposal. It is the patriotic duty of all of us to support this ally, and to invest in their future, at twenty-five per cent tax free per annum. *(Lots of 'hear hears')*

ALAN Thank you Mr Fletcher Dervish. Just the sort of chap this organisation needs as secretary. All in favour? *(All hands go up)*

PIERS Hold on, you only asked me to . . .

ALAN Unanimous, excellent. Piers Fletcher Dervish, come on down! *(Piers reluctantly takes the seat next to Alan, as all applaud)* Now, who's in for a fact-finding mission to the sunny Caribbean where the azure sea laps a golden beach, and the dusky maidens lap the visiting parliamentarians?

Virtually all put their hands up.

ALAN As many as that? Excellent, excellent. *(Looks at his papers)* The cost of the trip is only seven hundred and fifty-five pounds, including first class transportation, luxury accommodation, and a state reception hosted by President Okum-Martin, including a courtesy pina colada. Any questions?

FIDDICK Should we wish to . . . er . . . help the local tobacco industry, how do we go about depositing our money in the Bank of St James?

ALAN Speaking for myself, I will be taking a banker's draft for a hundred thousand pounds. It's as good as cash and a lot less bulky. *(Piers puts his hand up)* Piers?

PIERS Can my fiancée come?

ALAN If you don't know the answer to that one Piers, I suggest you call off the wedding. Now, if everyone would form an orderly queue . . .

Most of the people in the room move to the front and form a queue.

ALAN The Friends of St James honours all major gold credit cards . . . *(Takes one of those credit card machines out of his briefcase)*

9. EXT. DAKOTA AIRCRAFT. DAY.

Stock footage of an ancient piston-engined Dakota airliner, the sort that holds about forty passengers, we see it making a take-off (preferably a bumpy one) from Miami airport. In the background, blue skies and palm trees. We hear the following speech from the Captain, as a voice-over. He is a jovial Texan, ex-Vietnam, who once forgot to hold his breath when on a defoliation mission, and hasn't been quite the same since.

CAPTAIN   Well, sorry about the technical hitch folks, no-one's ever gotten any chewing gum when you need it. Still, we finally plugged the leak and we're airborne. My name is Bobby Hirsch, and I'm your Captain. Our flight time to Hanoi ... What? Sorry, our flight time to St James is approximately one hour. God bless you for flying Caribbean International Airways, God bless mom and dad, and God help President Reagan.

10. INT. DAKOTA CABIN. DAY.

Forty-five minutes later, inside the plane. About thirty British Members of Parliament sit in cramped seats, with large drinks on their little plastic tables. Only Alan and Piers, having secured the pair of seats by the entrance, have any leg room. As the party has already spent eight hours flying from London to Miami, two hours waiting in Miami, another hour on the tarmac in Miami waiting for someone to fix the fuel leak on this plane, everyone looks knackered, dishevelled and rather drunk.

PIERS   What an awful journey, I'm really knackered. *(Presses the recline button in the arm of his seat, and the seat collapses back into a horizontal position, with Piers falling back. Catchpole, sitting behind Piers, lets out a muffled squawk. Piers struggles out of the seat to release Catchpole, and returns the seat to its upright position)*

CATCHPOLE   *(Standing up drunkenly)* Bit cramped this plane, isn't it, B'stard?

ALAN   My words exactly. I should never have let Piers make the travel arrangements ...

PIERS   *(Weakly)* I didn't ... !

CATCHPOLE   You get more luxury on Aeroflot.

ALAN   Hear that, Piers? You're my witness. Labour front-bench spokesman admits he's a communist! Wait until the papers hear about that!

CATCHPOLE   Excuse me, must have a tinkle. *(Starts fumbling with an emergency exit door)*

PIERS   Why did you charter this old wreck?

ALAN   I chartered it, Piers, because it was extraordinarily cheap! We're ahead three hundred pounds per member before we even get to St James!

PIERS   *(Notices what Catchpole is doing)* Don't you think you should tell him that isn't the toilet?! Alan!!

ALAN   I face a moral dilemma here, Piers. On the one hand I'd like to see Comrade Catchpole hurtling out of the plane, but on the other hand I don't particularly wish to be sucked out after him. *(Raises his voice)* Catchpole ... *(Prods him with the toe of his shoe, Catchpole turns towards Alan)* I think there's someone in there, Tovarich.

CATCHPOLE   Oh ... *(Stumbles back to his seat)*

CAPTAIN   *(Voice from intercom)* Okay, we're about to commence our descent to St James. I hope you all've enjoyed the flight, because our motto is 'service with a smile'; that's why so many famous people have flown Caribbean International: Buddy Holly, Otis Redding, Jim Reeves, Glenn Miller . . . the old jokes are the best, folks! *(The plane suddenly hits some turbulence and Alan's drink goes all over his lap)* Wheeyoo! Ride 'em cowboy!

ALAN   *(Takes silk hankie from Piers's top pocket and mops up spilt drink)* God, I hate Americans! Their silly string ties, their revolting checked leezure-pants three inches too short, and their perpetual insincere 'Have a nice day!' How can you have a nice day when there are Americans around!? *(As he ends this tirade, he realises that standing over him is the curvy and desirable Cyndy, the stewardess)* Hello you beautiful American; I seem to have spilt my drink in my lap, perhaps you'd like to . . . mop it up?

CYNDY   I'd love to, but Captain Hirsch said could you come into the *(licks her lips)* cockpit right away?

Alan, somewhat puzzled, follows her through the flight deck door.

11. INT. FLIGHT DECK. DAY.

Continuous. On the cramped flight deck, we find Captain Hirsch and his co-pilot/navigator, Alex, in their respective seats. Cyndy shows Alan in, bats her eyelashes at Captain Hirsch, and goes.

CAPTAIN   Hi Al . . . Enjoying the flight?

ALAN   No.

CAPTAIN   Glad to hear it Al.

ALAN   Anything else?

CAPTAIN   Yup. Seems we got a little operational glitch relating to our ETA Al.

ALAN   In English?

CAPTAIN   It's kinda hard to explain, Al . . .

ALAN   Well break the habit of a lifetime, and use your brain.

CAPTAIN   Alex, demonstrate . . .

ALEX   *(Radios)* This is Caribbean International Airways, flight

001, requesting permission to land at St James International Airport.

Split screen with a corrugated iron hut on the island of St James. It is the police station. In it a couple of battered desks, and some rickety chairs. A ceiling fan turns slowly. A few black policemen lounge around, very mellow. One has sergeant's stripes, and operates the shortwave radio set. He replies to Alex's call.

SERGEANT   This is St James police station. Is that you again, man? You just won't take no for an answer! We tell you, the airstrip closed till we harvest the sugar cane, everyone know that.

ALAN   *(Snatching the microphone from Alex)* All right, listen to me. I am Alan B'Stard, Member of Parliament from England, my majority is four times the size of your entire pathetic population, and I'm visiting your island as the personal guest of President Okum-Martin, so stop playing silly black buggers!

SERGEANT   *(Laughs long and hard)* If President Lewis invited you, then praise the Lord, it's a miracle, the poor old guy bin deaf dumb and blind the last three years!

ALAN   President Lewis? What are you talking about?

SERGEANT   Lewis, that's the President's first name. We're all on first name terms here, this is a friendly island. Now push off, Honky!

ALAN   Listen, you stupid man, your President's name is Lance, he's perfectly fit and healthy . . . I should know, I went to school with him!

Alan is interrupted by a great burst of laughter from the sergeant.

SERGEANT   *(To his friends around him)* Sounds like Lance has taken another Honky for a ride. *(To Alan)* Lance is the President's grandson. He always pulling scams. Few years back, he nearly sold this entire island to the Disneyland people, that's what give the old man his stroke. Got out of bed one day, found Donald Duck in his swimming pool! Have a nice day.

End of split screen.

CAPTAIN   There you go, Al. Looks like you been well and truly shafted!

ALAN   And why didn't you know their airport was shut, you incompetent cowboy?!

CAPTAIN   *(With equanimity)* Well, between you me and the hitching post, Al, we ain't so familiar with this part of the world.

ALAN   Then what are you doing calling yourself Caribbean International Airways?

CAPTAIN   We gotta call ourselves something, Al . . .

ALAN   What about 'Crap In Action'? Same initials, save re-painting the plane.

CAPTAIN   Uh, see you've rumbled us, Al! You politicians don't miss a trick!

ALAN   *(Puzzled)* What?

CAPTAIN   *(Confidential wink)* Strictly entre noose, Al, we usually fly more in the Central American zone . . . We carry a lot of . . . bananas, to El Salvador. Catch my drift Al?

ALAN   Bananas to El Salvador!?! *(Captain winks)* Caribbean International Airways! You're the CIA! That explains why you're so bloody useless!

CAPTAIN   Win some, lose some, Al, that's what we say in the company. Shall we head back to Miami?

ALAN   *(Bitterly sarcastic)* No, it's such a nice day, and we are airborne: why don't we invade Cuba?

CAPTAIN   Now you're talking, Al!

ALAN   It was a joke.

12. INT. CABIN DAY.

Continuous. Alan returns to his seat.

ALAN   *(Really angry, mutters to himself)* . . . I'll kill that double-dealing, black con-merchant! He'll wish he was deaf, dumb and blind when I've finished with him!

PIERS   Something the matter Alan?

ALAN   Yes, the Bank of St James has had an attack of

premature liquidation ... *(Mind working overtime)* which means that you're in a lot of trouble, Piers!

PIERS Me!!?

ALAN You've taken over twenty thousand pounds from your parliamentary colleagues under false pretences.

PIERS But you've got the money!

ALAN I've got the money, but you're responsible for it, as treasurer of the Friends of St James.

PIERS I'm the secretary, not the treasurer!

ALAN Don't you try those double-dealing, cheese-paring, legalistic ploys with me, my learned friend! When these good people sober up and find out how you've swindled them, they'll throw you off the plane ... in mid-air!

PIERS Oh my God, I'm going to die, and I've never been physically intimate with my fiancée!

ALAN Well I have, and you aren't missing anything. Now, if you can get your mind off sex, I've just had a brilliant plan to save you! Give me your gold Rolex watch!

PIERS Why?

ALAN Because I've always wanted one, that's why! Can you believe it?! I'm about to save his miserable skin, and he's quibbling about a lousy watch! Keep it then, and time how long it takes you to hit the ground! I hope it's shock proof, that's all!

PIERS *(Removing watch)* No, I want you to have it!

ALAN Thank you Piers. *(Puts on watch, admires it on his wrist for a moment. Then ...)* Right, follow me!

Alan stands up, takes his flight bag from the overhead rack, and marches down the plane towards the toilet at the back, with Piers following. They pass row upon row of pickled parliamentarians. The toilet is engaged, Alan hammers on the door. After a second it opens, and Cyndy comes out, followed a few seconds later by a sheepish Catchpole.

ALAN The tabloids are going to have a field day with this, Catchpole! 'Communist Pervert In Sky High Hi-Jinks!' *(Alan waits until Catchpole returns to his seat, then enters the toilet. To Piers)* Come on! *(Piers follows him in, confused)*

13. INT. TOILET. DAY.

Continuous. The toilet is small and none too clean. Alan starts undressing.

ALAN   Get your clothes off . . .
PIERS   But we're not at public school any more!
ALAN   Come on, come on, no time to lose!

Alan has removed his shirt and tie, and opens his flight bag. Out of this he takes two T-shirts, and two pairs of Y-fronts. He sniffs both pairs and hands the smelly pair to Piers. Alan puts on his T-shirt, and pulls the pants over his head as a yashmak-like mask.

PIERS   What's going on?!
ALAN   We're going to hijack the plane, of course. *(Starts unscrewing the spherical, glass liquid-soap dispenser from the wall)*
PIERS   Oh, I see . . . What?! To where?
ALAN   Oh, I hadn't thought of where; hold on, I'll pop out and see if Judith Chalmers is on board, she'll know somewhere nice. *(Starts putting his other clothes into flight bag)* Now get changed!

14. INT. CABIN. DAY.

A couple of minutes later. The toilet door bursts open, and out charge Alan and Piers, both in T-shirts and Y-front masks. (Piers's T-shirt is far too small for him.) Alan has his flight bag slung over his shoulder. Cyndy is canoodling with another couple of MPs.

CYNDY   . . . Yes, I took a Master's in political science at Cornell, but it doesn't do to come over too smart in this line of business . . . *(Alan grabs her)* Eek!

Alan holds Cyndy in front of him, very tightly with one arm, while holding up the soap dispenser like a grenade.

ALAN   *(Top of his voice, in a Spanish accent)* Okay, this plane is being hijacked by the People's Liberation Army of St James. *(Passengers start to turn around)* Nobody turn round! We have grenades!

CYNDY   Do what he says! He's got a gun pressed into my back!

ALAN   *(His face shows it isn't a gun, but he's flattered Cyndy thinks it is)* Everyone put their heads between their knees! *(They all do. S/V to Piers)* God, they did! If one of you gringo pigs looks up, you're all Lassie Meaty Chunks, enriched with nourishing Member of Parliament!

CATCHPOLE   You can't kill me, I'm a Socialist. I'm on your side!

ALAN   *(Screams)* You're a socialist? I'm a fascist!

CATCHPOLE   *(Moans)* Oh God!

ALAN   Okay, you will all remove your wallets and pass them to Comrade Juan. *(S/V to Piers)* That's you . . .

Piers reluctantly starts to make his way along the aisle. To his surprise, every member quickly passes his wallet, without looking up. Piers finds a flight bag to carry the wallets in. As he collects the wallets, Alan walks alongside, still holding on to Cyndy.

ALAN   Quickly, you decadent pigs, if you wish to see another dawn! We will avenge the martyrs of the Battle of San . . . San Ilav!

PIERS   *(S/V to Alan)* Sanilav!?

ALAN   *(S/V to Piers)* My mind just went blank for a second, now I know how you feel all the time. *(By now, Alan and Piers and the reluctant Cyndy have moved to the front of the plane. Alan gives the 'grenade' to Piers, takes the bag of wallets, and, still clasping Cyndy, opens door to go through to flight deck)* Long live the glorious October the Thirteenth Movement! *(Exits)*

PIERS   *(To himself)* October the thirteenth? Isn't that Mrs Thatcher's birthday?

15. INT. FLIGHT DECK. DAY.

Continuous. Alan bursts in with Cyndy. Captain Hirsch and Alex are piloting the plane. They turn.

CAPTAIN Jesus Christ!! *(Jumps up, producing a magnum − not of champagne − from inside his flight jacket)*

ALAN *(Ripping off his mask)* It's okay, it's okay, it's me! *(Let Cyndy go)*

CAPTAIN What in the name of Ronald H. Reagan is going on, Al?!

ALAN It's far too complicated for an American to follow. Look, I'll give you all the cash in this bag to forget this ever happened.

CAPTAIN Deal, Al.

ALAN *(Quickly going through wallets, Alan separates a pile of bank notes and a pile of banker's drafts)* . . . And I'll just hang on to all these lovely banker's drafts . . . Now, if you'd be so kind as to turn on the intercom . . . *(Captain does so. Alan puts on his hijacker voice)* Fly this plane to Cuba or I will blow the head off this English capitalist pig!

In the cabin, the cowed MPs hear Alan's response.

ALAN   *(Own voice)* Don't listen to him, Captain Hirsch, he's bluffing!

On the flight deck.

ALAN   *(Hijacker's voice)* Fly to Cuba, or we all die! This grenade is primed, I have only to remove my finger . . . !

CAPTAIN   *(To Alex and Cyndy, S/V)* This guy's good. *(Aloud)* I'm taking a course for Cuba, comrade. Don't kill us!

CYNDY   *(Entering into the spirit)* I'll do anything, just don't move your finger!

In the cabin Piers stands over cowed MPs with the soap dispender grenade, but the drama being played out over the loudspeaker enthrals him.

PIERS   *(To himself)* I hope Alan's all right in there with that maniac!

ALAN   *(Own voice over loudspeaker)* Uhhh! Nnh! Quick, Captain, I've got the grenade! Grab them! *(Hijack voice)* You will never take us alive! Come, Juan, jump . . . ! *(Own voice)* God, no, the emergency exit! *(Hijack voice)* For the glory of the revolution! *(Dying fall)* Aaaaaahhhh! *(Own voice)* See that, Captain? One of the blighters has got a parachute!

Then Alan's arm comes out of the flight deck door and pulls Piers through into the flight deck.

ALAN   *(S/V to Captain)* Is the intercom off? *(Captain nods)* Quick Piers, get changed! *(Alan rips off T-shirt, puts own shirt back on, then rips a couple of holes in the shirt. Piers also gets his shirt on)* Now hit me.

PIERS   Why?

ALAN   I need some sign of my heroic fight. *(Piers punches him in the face, rather harder than Alan had anticipated)* I'll get you for that! *(To Captain)* Okay, Bobby . . .

16. INT. CABIN. DAY.

Continuous. Most of the passengers are still too frightened to look up. One or two are beginning to warily do so. (Though one or two older members have dozed off.) Then the Captain comes into the cabin.

CAPTAIN   It's okay, folks, it's all over, thanks to your Mr B'Stard. I knew some brave men in 'Nam, but this guy makes Rambo look like Sylvester Stallone!

Alan comes out of the flightdeck, as relieved MPs straighten up. He has a bloody nose. The MPs give him a tumultuous round of applause. Piers sneaks back into his seat without being spotted. Alan holds his hands up for silence.

ALAN   Thank you, it's all right, I only did my duty. After all, I brought you out here. *(False regret)* I'm just sorry things went so drastically wrong, obviously St James is not a safe investment prospect. *(Cries of 'Not your fault' and 'Well done B'Stard')* I'm afraid that when I overpowered the hijackers and they parachuted out of the plane, they took all our wallets with them! So all the banker's drafts we brought to deposit in St James are now in the hands of desperate terrorists.

CATCHPOLE   To hell with the money, you're a hero, B'Stard!

OTHER MEMBERS   – That's right, you've saved our lives! – The money doesn't matter. – Thank God we're safe!

Alan basks in the adulation.

PIERS   *(Has been briefed by Alan)* Anyway, we're all insured, aren't we? *(Reaction shows some were, some weren't)*

ALAN   *(Regretfully)* I didn't take out any insurance, I was so confident . . . well, that's a hundred thousand down the drain . . .

PIERS   We can't let Alan lose all that, can we? I propose we have a collection for him when we get back. All in favour? *(Most hands go up at once, the others follow suit)*

ALAN   Thank you, I'm very touched . . . *(Sits with Piers in their old seats)* If the collection tops ten grand you can have your watch back.

Three-Line Whipping

1. EXT. A FINE LONDON SQUARE. DAY.

About 8.30 on a June evening, still light. A lovely Georgian Square. A taxi draws up outside a large and respectable town house, and Alan gets out. He wears a smart lightweight suit and dark glasses. Perhaps he's trying to remain anonymous. He pays the cabbie, goes up to the front door of the house, and rings the doorbell. By the way, the house is a brothel.

2. INT. BROTHEL HALL. DAY.

Continuous. The beautiful hall of the brothel. It must not look like a house of ill-repute. It is beautifully decorated, in perfect taste. Mrs Selway, the Madam, responds to the bell and opens the door. She is about forty-five, beautifully spoken, and also is decorated in the best possible taste. She doesn't seem at all like a Madam. Rather, it should seem as if Alan is coming to a respectable dinner party.

MRS SELWAY My dear, how delightful, I'm so pleased you could find the time . . .

ALAN   *(Kissing her on both cheeks, French style)* My pleasure absolutely, Mrs Selway . . .

MRS SELWAY   And how is your lovely wife?

ALAN   No idea, haven't seen her for days.

MRS SELWAY   It's not easy to make a marriage work these days, but I can see you have the secret. I've put you in the pink room . . .

ALAN   My favourite.

3. INT. PINK ROOM. DAY.

A lovely Georgian bedroom, featuring four-poster bed, with everything decorated in shades of pink. The festoon blinds are down, and the light is subtle. There's a small TV on a bedside table. Alan enters. A young tart, Chantelle, is sitting on the bed, decorously watching TV. She's about twenty, and quite pretty. She wears a teacher's gown over her Janet Reger basque, and a mortar board is perched pertly on her head. She turns off the TV as Alan enters. Her accent suggests she comes from Morecambe rather than Marseilles.

ALAN   *(Likes the look of her)* Hello . . .

CHANTELLE   Bonjour, my name's Chantelle, I'm your new French mistress . . . You must be Mr B?

ALAN   Yes, but please call me Piers . . .

CHANTELLE   That's a nice name . . .

ALAN   Yes. It isn't mine, of course . . .

CHANTELLE   Me neither . . . *(As Alan takes off his jacket and starts to undo his shirt)* Mrs Selway told me what you like . . . you naughty boy!

ALAN   I find it helps me unwind after a long sitting . . . *(There's a rack of whips and canes next to the bed. Alan crosses to it, picks out a very whippy cane)* Mmm, this is a nice whippy one . . . *(Puts cane on bed, and takes off his shoes and trousers)*

CHANTELLE   I told you what would happen if you failed your French oral again . . . *(As Alan bends over to take off his socks, Chantelle picks up the cane and gives Alan two or three hard swipes on the bum)*

ALAN   What?! Jesus!! Ouch!! *(She swipes him again. He retreats around the bed. She chases him with her cane)* That hurts! Stop it!

CHANTELLE   It's meant to hurt, you wicked boy!

Alan grabs hold of her arm to stop her hitting him again, and punches her in the face.

ALAN   You stupid trollop! I'm not a masochist, I'm a sadist! I pay to beat you!

CHANTELLE   *(Crying)* I'm sorry, I'm new here!

4. EXT. BROTHEL. DAY.

Early the following morning. It is already light, but very quiet. A milk float goes down the road. Inspector Radford, a uniformed policeman, goes up to Mrs Selway's front door. Several other uniformed policemen and women wait a few yards behind him. He knocks on the door. Mrs Selway opens it. He rushes in, knocking her to one side. His coppers follow.

5. INT. PINK ROOM. DAY.

Meanwhile . . . Alan is lying on his stomach, in bed asleep. Chantelle is nowhere to be seen. There are heavy footsteps on the stairs, the door bursts open, and Inspector Radford enters, with a uniformed sergeant.

RADFORD　Here, this one's got more stripes than you, Sarge! *(As Alan stirs)* All right, you pervert! Downstairs, now! *(Sergeant goes to get Alan out of bed as Radford exits)*

6. INT. BROTHEL HALL. DAY.

A few minutes later. Several men, mostly much older than Alan, have been herded together in the hall. They all have sheets or towels round them. Three or four uniformed coppers stand guard over them. The sergeant from the previous scene ushers Alan to join them.

ALAN　*(To no-one in particular)* I shouldn't be here at all. I'm from the *Good Food Guide*. Terrible mix up at the office . . .

Oddly, the other clients seem more annoyed than frightened by the raid. One addresses Alan.

JUDGE　What a damn bore these interruptions are . . . takes me long enough to get my engine running as it is . . .

ALAN　*(Sizing Judge up)* Yes, it must be pretty clapped out, if the bodywork's anything to go by.

POLICE COMMANDER *(Spotting Judge)* Cyril, I didn't know you were a member here, old boy!

JUDGE Yes, I've been coming here for years, the girlies are so fragrant . . .

POLICE COMMANDER So to speak . . . *(Both laugh)* Congrats on your Knighthood, by the way . . .

JUDGE Well, strictly between Freemasons, I'd been told I was onto a 'K', if the jury found that randy little politician not guilty on the kerb-crawling charge.

POLICE COMMANDER Was he guilty?

JUDGE As it happens, no . . . he was here at the time, I saw him . . .

POLICE COMMANDER *(Laughs, then recognises Alan)* Hello, it's B'Stard, isn't it?

ALAN   *(Cautiously)* Not necessarily . . .

POLICE COMMANDER   Yes, course it is! You did jolly well with your private member's Bill arming the police . . .

At this moment, an agitated Mrs Selway appears from within, accompanied by Inspector Radford.

MRS SELWAY   *(To clients)* I'm most terribly sorry, gentlemen! Inspector Radford here is new, and apparently no-one has explained our special relationship with the local force . . .

RADFORD   If you're implying *(Heavy 'wit')* Madam, that some nod and wink deal has been in operation between my nick and your bawdy house . . . !?

MRS SELWAY   Of course it has! It's been that way for years . . . !

RADFORD   You realise I could do you for that?!

ALAN   And I expect she'd give you a discount . . .

RADFORD   *(Scowls at Alan, then, to clients in general)* All right, sleazebags, names and addresses . . . *(Gets out note book)*

JUDGE   Right Honourable Sir Cyril Haversham-Armstrong, Court of Appeal . . . And this is *(Indicating General)* Major General Ralph Murdo McDonald, KCMG, KCVO, DSO – Ministry of Defence . . .

RADFORD   *(Stops writing names down)* If you think I'm going to waste ink writing down this crap . . . ! *(To Alan)* Now, let's have your readl name!

ALAN   Piers Fletcher Dervish MP, House of Commons . . .

RADFORD   I'm warning you . . . !!

POLICE COMMANDER   Before you go on, Inspector, let me show you this. *(He has boxer shorts on, and he puts his hand in the waistband)* My warrant card. *(Offers it to Radford)*

RADFORD   *(Reads)* Commander Stapleton, Vice Squad! *(Limply hands warrant card back)* That'll do nicely, sir. *(To his coppers)* All right, lads, there seems to have been an administrative cock-up here . . .

ALAN   What a facility you have for the telling phrase, Inspector.

7. INT. PINK ROOM. DAY.

Moments later, Alan enters, and sits gingerly on the bed. No sign of Chantelle, so he switches on the television. On the TV Good Morning Britain *(TV AM) has just started, and Anne Diamond is previewing the morning's show. Alan starts to climb back into bed.*

ANNE ... And in a few minutes we'll have Bob Crippen MP and Alan B'Stard MP in the studio to discuss the implications of last night's crucial by-election. But first, Popeye ...

ALAN *(Having almost dozed off, realises what Anne has said)* Oh SHIT! *(Jumps out of bed, rushes across to the wardrobe, opens it. In it is his suit, also in it is Chantelle, bound and gagged and with a black eye)*

CHANTELLE Hmpphh hmmphh!!

ALAN That'll teach you to beat up your clients! *(Shuts wardrobe)*

8. EXT. BROTHEL. DAY.

A few minutes later, Alan hurtles down the front steps of the knocking shop. He has dressed hastily, hasn't shaved, and looks rough. He looks around desperately for a cab. One or two go by, occupied. Then he sees a vacant cab pass him. He waves an arm, and the taxi stops a couple of dozen yards away. Alan sprints to the cab.

ALAN TV AM, double double quick!

CABBY *(Jocosely)* I hope you're not asking me to exceed the speed limit, sir?

ALAN Just bloody well drive!! *(Gets in. Cab drives off sedately)*

9. INT. TAXI DAY.

Inside the taxi, Alan perched uncomfortably on the seat. The taxi goes at a stately pace through quiet streets towards TV AM, in Camden Town.

CABBY   *(Over shoulder to Alan)* Sit well back in your seat if you wouldn't mind, chief, in case I have to do an emergency stop . . .

ALAN   I'll sit as I choose! Just mind your own business and put your horribly common foot down!

Cabby pulls into the side of the road and applies the handbrake.

CABBY   The Metropolitan Hackney Carriage office would have my badge if I didn't attend to passengers' safety at all time . . .

ALAN   All right, I'm sitting comfortably *(Sits well back)* now will you begin, you irritating little virus!?

The cabby drives slowly off.

CABBY   I know why you were perching on the edge of your seat! You've been for a bit of hanky spanky at Mrs Selway's famous knocking emporium! *(Alan slams the partition window shut. Cabby reopens it)* Nothing to be ashamed of, Mrs Selway's place is a landmark of old London. It's even one of the runs on *the Knowledge* now; how do you get from Mrs Selway's to the Middlesex Hospital Clap Clinic . . .

10. EXT. TV AM. DAY.

Ten minutes later. The cab reaches TV AM, and pulls into the forecourt. Alan gets out and rushes into the building without paying his fare.

CABBY   *(Calls)* Oy! I didn't expect a tip, but . . .

11. INT. TV AM STUDIO. DAY.

A floor assistant brings Alan straight onto the set of Good Morning Britain. *Jane is on the sofa. Bob Crippen is already in the studio, smoking a fag. On the monitor, we can see an ad break.*

CRIPPEN You're cutting it fine, B'Stard . . . whose bed did you oversleep in then?

FLOOR MANAGER *(Getting a message through earpiece, turns to Alan)* You're on right after the break . . . is there anything you need?

ALAN More cushions . . .

The floor manager sends the floor assistant for a cushion. A make-up girl comes to Alan and makes the best of a bad job. Floor assistant returns with cushion which Alan slides under his sore botty. The floor manager gives the five-second count-down with his fingers. Crippen stubs out his fag.

ALAN *(Sudden panic, grabs floor assistant's arm as he passes)* Who won the by-election?!

FLOOR MANAGER What by-election?

JANE Yesterday's by-election posed an important challenge to all political parties. In the studio this morning we have Alan B'Stard, Conservative MP for Haltemprice, and Bob Crippen, Labour Member for Bramall. *(Turns to Alan)* Well, Alan, all the pundits said that this by-election, in a key Tory marginal, would be an important hurdle for the Government. Were you surprised by the result?

ALAN *(Decides Jane's question means the Government has lost the seat. He leans forward, looking very confident − though in fact, his posture is designed to keep the bulk of his bum off the sofa)* Not really . . . were you surprised by the result Bob?

CRIPPEN *(Taken aback at being addressed Bob)* Surprised? I was completely gobstruck! It was a bolt from the blue!

ALAN Of course it was, but a predictable one.

JANE But to get down to specifics . . .

ALAN Look Jane, I think people have had enough of politics this year. Let us talk about what really matters; how is Ann Diamond's lovely little baby doing?

CRIPPEN We're here to talk about the by-election result not some media brat . . . unless you don't know the result, B'Stard!?

ALAN I not know the result! That's outrageous!

CRIPPEN   What was it then?

ALAN   I'm not going to be browbeaten by some bald-headed
crypto-Stalinist!

CRIPPEN   All right, you ask him Jane.

JANE   I'm sure you *must* know the result, Alan?

ALAN   Yes, of course . . . Labour . . . *(The other two laugh)* . . .
came second, and we held the seat, of course. It was a
foregone conclusion . . .

JANE   Actually, it was a surprise victory for the SDP . . .

ALAN   I don't believe it, they're more split than Arthur Scar-
gill's personality! *(Gets up)* And you wouldn't be asking me
these difficult questions if I had a book to plug! *(Unclips
microphone, throws it to the floor and storms off set)*

CRIPPEN   Don't Mrs Selway have a newspaper delivered?

JANE   Who's Mrs Selway?

12. INT. TOILET. DAY.

*Moments later, a deflated Alan enters the 'Gents' at TV AM.
The floor manager is just rezipping after a tinkle. He supresses a
laugh and exits. Alan looks gloomily at his face in the mirror.
Then the door opens again and in comes the cabby. He is four feet
tall.*

CABBY   Oy oy! Now I know what MP stands for −
Monumental Prat!

ALAN   *(Angrily turns round, and doesn't immediately see cabby, who
is below his eye line. Then he realises who it is)* How dare you,
you little . . . !

CABBY   *(Going to urinal)* Heightist! I had to hang about, you
didn't pay my fare, so I came in and watched you on the set in
reception; it was worth £3.50 of anybody's money, so the
ride's on me. *(Gives it a shake)* Blimey, I feel almost sorry for
you, when She finds out about this morning, I shouldn't be
surprised if there's a by-election called in your constituency!

ALAN   Shut up!

CABBY   Fancy not even knowing the result! I'd have told you if
you'd asked me nicely. But you didn't want to hear my vulgar
northern accent . . .

ALAN   Shut up, or I'll hit you!

CABBY   Oh, yeah, very brave, hit a man of diminished stature,
with a dicky heart to boot! Just goes to show, any old tosspot
can become a Tory MP if he knows what palms to grease!

ALAN   *(Quivering with rage)* I'm warning you!

CABBY   I've always wanted to meet a surviving brain transplant
donor . . .

ALAN   That does it!!! *(Picks cabby up by lapels to Alan's eye level,
and slams him into the hard tiled wall. The cabby instantly glazes
into unconsciousness, and a shocked Alan lets him slide down the
wall onto the floor, leaving a trail of blood on the white tiles)* Come
on, get up, you pinko runt! *(Cabby does not stir. Worry replaces
rage on Alan's face. He crouches down and puts his ear to cabby's
chest)* Oh, Christ, that's all I need first thing on a Friday
morning! A dead dwarf!

13. EXT. TV AM. DAY.

A few minutes later. A ground floor toilet window, with frosted glass, opens. Alan peers out. The coast is clear. He climbs out of the window. The cab is parked a few yards away. Alan drags the cabby's corpse out behind him, and swiftly conveys it to the cab. He opens the boot and crams the body in. He removes the cabby's keys from cabby's pocket, shuts the boot, and gets into the driver's seat. He manages to start up the cab, and pulls gingerly out of the forecourt, and into the street. The 'For Hire' sign is on and he doesn't know how to turn it off. Several people hail him as he drives away, but he ignores them. But when he is forced to stop at a red light, a businessman comes to Alan's window.

BUSINESSMAN   Albert Hall . . .

ALAN   Fred Housego, pleased to meet you . . . *(Lights change, Alan speeds off from bemused businessman)*

14. INT. ALAN'S OFFICE. DAY.

Half an hour later. Alan wearily enters his office. Piers and Sir Stephen are there, and look bleary from an all night sitting.

PIERS   Oh, do I know you? Yes, it's Alan thingy, isn't it . . . ?

ALAN   Spare me your pathetic attempts at wit, Piers! *(Sits heavily in his chair)*

SIR STEPHEN   And where were you last night when we were voting on the Bill to recriminalise prostitution?

ALAN   I was paired . . .

SIR STEPHEN   Yes, with one of Mrs Selway's girls, no doubt! Hypocrite!

ALAN   Au contraire, I'd only be a hypocrite if I had voted last night. I like brothels; you don't have to pretend to respect women.

PIERS   The Chief Whip's out for your blood, you know . . .

SIR STEPHEN   And everyone's talking about what an arse you made of yourself on television this morning. You've let us all down, B'Stard. I'm disappointed in you.

ALAN Do you think I give an orang-utang's for the opinion of a man with a plastic drainpipe where his colon should be?

SIR STEPHEN *(Hurt)* You'll be old too one day, B'Stard.

ALAN But I shan't be bionic. *(Sir Stephen exits with remains of his dignity)* Off to his Harley Street plumber, no doubt. *(Turns to Piers)* Piers, will you do me a small favour?

PIERS *(Cagey)* That depends . . .

ALAN I've got a taxi waiting downstairs . . .

PIERS And you want me to go and pay the driver, as usual . . .

ALAN Don't try to anticipate me, you haven't the wit. I want you to drive the taxi out into the country, somewhere secluded, and set fire to it.

PIERS *(Amazed)* Why?!

ALAN Because it's a very old taxi and I don't need it any more. Here are the keys . . .

PIERS I don't want to.

ALAN What? Why not?! Give me one good reason?!

PIERS *(Weakly)* I've been up all night . . .

ALAN I see. Well, if you won't do a simple favour for your best friend . . . !

PIERS I wouldn't call setting fire to a taxi exactly a simple favour . . .

ALAN Of course it's simple, it's as simple as you! All it takes is a can of petrol and a box of matches! Never mind, I'll do it myself! Give me your wallet!

PIERS Why?

ALAN You don't expect me to pay my own fare back from the middle of nowhere after I've disposed of the taxi for you?!

PIERS Oh, sorry Alan. *(Hands him his wallet)*

ALAN That's better. *(Picks Piers's Barbour waxed jacket off the coat-rack)* Is this yours, Piers?

PIERS *(Proudly)* Yes, it's new . . . do you want to borrow it?

ALAN Waterproof, is it?

PIERS Yes, it's impregnated with wax . . .

ALAN *(Opens window and throws coat out)* Let's see how it copes with Old Father Thames.

15. EXT. SOUTHWARK STREET. DAY.

Ten minutes later. Alan driving along in cab, with 'For Hire' sign on, but ignoring people hailing him. Then a policeman steps out into the middle of the road and forces him to stop. At the side of the road is a black Jaguar, which has had a minor collision with another car. There are three people in the back of the Jaguar — one of them is clearly Margaret Thatcher.

ALAN *(Trying not to panic)* Yes, officer?

OFFICER Dulwich . . .

The police officer waves over to the Jag. The PM's detective — a burly, plain clothes bodyguard — gets out and escorts her and a male colleague, the Chief Whip, over to Alan's taxi. The three of them get in. Alan drives off. He looks a very worried man.

16. INT. TAXI. DAY.

The taxi is driving through south London on the way to Dulwich. If at all possible this scene should be shot in the studio. Alan is hunched into his muffler, terrified he is going to be recognised. The PM is chatting to her Chief Whip about Alan's TV appearance. The detective is perched on one of the flip down seats looking vigilant.

CHIEF WHIP . . . And how does Dennis react to the idea of your running for a fourth term?

PM He's less than completely enamoured. Threatening to vote Monster Raving Loony . . .

CHIEF WHIP Mind you, many more Tory performances like B'Stard's this morning and there may not be a fourth . . .

PM *(Interrupting)* Yes, what are we going to do about him, Chief Whip? It was quite the worst television appearance by a politician since Michael Foot hung up his welding spectacles.

CHIEF WHIP And he failed to respond to a three-line whip last night! He seems to think that just because he's got the largest majority in the House, he's immune to discipline! Well, tomorrow I intend to haul him over the coals . . .

ALAN *(Affecting a northern accent and going for broke)* Pardon the intrusion, but I saw him on telly this morning, and I think he did champion!

CHIEF WHIP Do you mind?!! I don't believe the Prime Minister intended to include you in her conversation . . . *(Goes to close the divider)*

PM No, I'm interested in hearing what the man in the street has to say . . .

ALAN And you're in the right place, ma'am, cos the man in the street frequently becomes the man in my cab. In fact, you're being driven by a one-man opinion poll! And seventy-two per cent of my passengers say that Alan B'Stard's all right! He speaks his mind, says what us decent working chaps *(Corrects himself)* er folk, want to hear. I mean, didn't he get that law through what give the police their guns? Right! Granted he seemed a bit nervy on the telly this morning, but I reckon he was just trying to wind that commie Crippen up!

CHIEF WHIP *(Patronising)* Thank you for sharing your political insights with us . . . *(Shuts divider)* Now, about the committee arrangements . . .

ALAN *(Opens divider)* I've always been Labour in the past, never cared for them old fashioned toffee-nosed Tories like that Sir Stephen Baxter! But with ordinary lads like B'Stard coming through, you'll get my vote, and hundreds of other cabbies feel the same way . . .

17. EXT. SUBURBAN STREET. DAY.

Long shot of taxi driving along, with Alan's voice over.

ALAN . . . And your B'Stard said 'If our nippers want to sing "Baa baa black sheep," what right has some darkie teacher with a tea cosy on his head to tell them they're racist . . . ?' Brilliant, what a card!

CHIEF WHIP We'd have got more work done if we'd taken a bus!

18. EXT. DULWICH. DAY.

A few minutes later, the taxi pulls up behind Dennis's Roller, outside a new Queen Anne-style detached house. The three passengers get out, and the detective gets out his wallet. Then sees 'For Hire' sign has not been turned off.

DETECTIVE   Oy, Mouthie, you know it's illegal to pick up fares without turning your meter on?

ALAN   Fares? I wouldn't charge that wonderful woman a brass farthing, even if my family was starving, which of course it isn't, because us small business folk are flourishing under her wise government!

DETECTIVE   *(Puts wallet away)* Crawler. *(Turns away towards house)*

ALAN   *(Shouts)* That doesn't mean I weren't expecting a decent tip!! *(But the Thatcher party goes into house without looking back)* I think that's thrown her off the scent.

19. EXT. COUNTRY LANE. DAY.

About an hour later, and Alan has finally driven out beyond London. We see the cab proceeding down a lonely lane, with Alan looking for somewhere to dispose of the cab.

20. INT. TAXI. DAY.

Continuous.

ALAN   Must be somewhere round here a chap can set fire to a taxi! *(Sees a track leading away from the road. Turns into it)* This'll do!

21. EXT. TRACK. DAY.

Alan drives down the track, stops, gets out. There is plenty of cover, and no-one seems to be about. He gets a gallon can of petrol out of the passenger compartment of the cab. He pours some over the bonnet. Then he hears a sound. He looks around. A man on horseback has appeared, and is watching him.

ALAN Can't bear to have a dirty bonnet. *(Gets out hankie, starts polishing, as if the petrol he poured over cab was actually Turtle Wax)*

22. EXT. COUNTRY LANE. DAY.

Alan driving along some more. There is a lake coming up. Alan turns off the road and drives up to the edge of the lake. There is a sign that says: 'Deep water, no lifeguard on duty.' Alan takes handbrake off, gets out, and starts pushing taxi towards water's edge. Suddenly, a woman on a windsurfer sails into view and nears Alan. Alan opens the bonnet.

ALAN Overheating . . . got to wait for it to cool down before I can top up the radiator. *(The woman sails off, not really interested)*

23. EXT. COUNTRY LANE. DAY.

The taxi driving down another lane!

24. INT. TAXI. DAY.

Continuous. Alan is cross and tired.

ALAN Stupid, over-populated county! In Yorkshire it'd be a piece of pudding! *(He yawns, looks at watch, and loses control of taxi!)*

25. EXT. COUNTRY LANE. DAY.

Continuous. We see the taxi career into a ditch.

ALAN *(O.O.V.)* Aaahh!

26. INT. TAXI. DAY.

*Continuous. Alan's seat belt has protected him from harm, except
that he has banged his head and now has a satisfactory trickle of
blood running down his face. He is delighted. He gets out of the
driver's seat, sees there's no-one around, and goes to the boot. He
opens it, and pulls the cabby's body out. He drags the body round
to the front of the taxi, and props it in the driver's seat. Alan
then gets into the back of the cab, arranges himself on the floor of
the cab in an unconscious position, and waits to be discovered.*

27. INT. TAXI. NIGHT.

*Several hours later, and it's dark. Alan has fallen asleep on the
floor of the cab. Then we see a blue flashing light through the
window of the taxi, and hear a police siren. Alan wakes up, looks
out of the window, then at watch.*

ALAN   About time! *(Resumes the unconscious position)*

28. EXT. TAXI. NIGHT.

*(In the studio) The police car stops next to the taxi, with blue
lights flashing. Two patrolmen get out, one goes to the driver, one
looks into the passenger compartment. Of course the patrolmen
have pistols at their waists.*

The passenger door opens and patrolman 1 looks in.

PATROLMAN 1   Are you all right, sir?
ALAN   Nnnhh . . .
PATROLMAN 1   Here . . . *(Waves smelling salts under Alan's
   nose)*
ALAN   Mnn, no, no more gorgonzola for me, I'm stuffed . . .
PATROLMAN 1   *(Calls)* This one's coming round . . .
PATROLMAN 2   *(O.O.V.)* The ambulance is here . . .

29. EXT. COUNTRY LANE. NIGHT.

We see the ambulance pulling up behind the police car, which is behind the cab. The ambulance crew, a man and a woman, jump out. As they do so, they see Alan getting shakily out of the cab.

PATROLMAN 2   Over here . . .

The ambulance people hurry over to where patrolman 2 crouches concernedly next to apparently dead cabby. Meanwhile, Alan is giving a statement to patrolman 1.

ALAN   I was at TV AM . . .

PATROLMAN 1   I thought it was you! *(Tries not to laugh)*

ALAN   *(Glares at patrolman)* I finished my interview, and asked him to take me back to my Chelsea pied-à-terre. Suddenly he went mad, started driving through red lights, shouting and cursing me and the Conservative Party! I tried to throw myself out, but there are child locks on the doors! He was obviously insane . . . and now he's dead . . . Better I suppose than life in a lunatic asylum . . .

AMBULANCE PERSON *(Tending cabby)* I think this one's going to be all right too!

ALAN What?!

CABBY *(Coming round, sees Alan)* There he is! There's the sodding maniac! He tried to kill me! *(Tries to get at Alan, but is easily restrained by patrolman 2)*

PATROLMAN 2 Now take it easy, shorty, you're still concussed . . .

CABBY And look at the state of my cab!!

PATROLMAN 1 All right, all right! Come on, let's all get back to the nick, and sort it out there . . .

ALAN There's nothing to sort out officer. You have my statement. Who are you going to believe? The Conservative Member of Parliament with the largest majority in the House of Commons, or this foul-mouthed, ignorant, stunted little taxi driver? If I were you, I would take this homunculus back to the police station — and have him tested for drugs!

The two patrolmen look at each other, then look at Alan, then at the cabby. They reach wordless agreement, and pick cabby up by the armpits. They march him to the patrol car, his legs thrashing in the air.

CABBY What do you think you're doing to me?! You can't believe all that old bollocks! *(The patrolmen force him into the car, cutting off the sound of his tirade, though we can see his mouth opening and closing through the window)*

AMBULANCE PERSON *(Taking Alan's arm)* If you'd like to come with us, sir, we'll take you to Basildon General, get that wound dressed.

ALAN You don't think I'd set foot inside a National Health Service hospital after ten years of Government cut-backs?! Take me to Harley Street!

30. INT. OFFICE. DAY.

Following day. Alan enters the office. Sir Stephen is there, looking superior.

SIR STEPHEN Ah, B'Stard! Come to clear your desk out, have you?

ALAN What?

SIR STEPHEN The Chief Whip was in here earlier, looking for you . . . but you weren't here. That's three times you've let him down in two days . . . He left muttering about breaches of discipline. If I were you I would try to land a few directorships whilst you still have MP after your name.

ALAN But I've got the biggest majority in the House. What can he do to me?

SIR STEPHEN   He can have you thrown out of the Party; he can promote you and send you to Ulster. He can . . .

The Chief Whip enters. Sir Stephen shuts up.

ALAN   Ah, Chief Whip, just the man . . . Perhaps you can give me some advice? I've just been left twenty thousand pounds by a distant aunt, and fortunately, as I'm extremely wealthy, and I don't need the money, I've decided to donate it to your favourite charity. And being an anti-bureaucratic type of chap, I thought 'cut out the red tape, give it to the good old Chief Whip in his hand, and let him get on with it' . . .

CHIEF WHIP   *(Obviously in a mood)* Cut the crap, B'Stard. I don't like you, I've never liked you, and I don't wish to spend any more time in your company than is absolutely necessary. I think your behaviour over the last days has been execrable, and if it were up to me, you'd become an unfortunate hiccough in the otherwise downward trend of the unemployment statistics. The Prime Minister, however, seems to rather like you. I suppose even the greatest Post War Leader this country has had is entitled to one lapse of judgement.

SIR STEPHEN   *(Aghast)* She likes him!!?

CHIEF WHIP   I'm afraid so . . . I do wish she wouldn't keep talking to taxi drivers.

ALAN   *(In cabby voice)* I don't know, happen it's good for her to keep in touch with the man in the street . . . *(The Chief Whip does a horrified double take. Alan grins)*

Live from Westminster Palace

1. INT. COMMONS CHAMBER. DAY.

The Commons is quite full and getting fuller. There is a theatrical atmosphere. It's day one of the televising of the House of Commons. There are TV lights and cables everywhere, and technicians and make-up girls bustle about. Lots of people in jeans and headphones with walkie-talkies disrupting the tenor of the place. Cameras, both conventional and hand-held, swoop around the chamber. Meanwhile, a debate is actually taking place, and a minister is making a speech, playing to the cameras.

MINISTER ... And this Government believes the choice lies between military conscription and corporal punishment ...

We fade the Minister to background, and move in on the back bench where Piers and Sir Stephen sit. Sir Stephen wears his 'formals', but Piers is dressed in territorial army combat fatigues − flak jacket, trousers, beret, and boots, and with smears of black camouflage paint on his face.

SIR STEPHEN *(Jumps up)* Mr Speaker, on a point of procedure ... !

PIERS Sir Stephen, that's not in the script!

SIR STEPHEN *(Startled, sits)* Script?!

PIERS *(Takes some pink pages from jacket pocket and gives them to Sir Stephen)* Whenever a Labour man gets up we have to go 'Wha-wha-wha-wooh'! *(Makes typical parliamentary farmyard noises)* And whenever a Labour man stumbles over his words we have to shout 'Hah-hah-hah'! And if one of us speaks, it's 'Hearhearhearhear' . . . there's nothing about points of procedure . . .

SIR STEPHEN Ye Gods and little fishes, that it should come to this! The temple of democracy desecrated by television cameras! The forum of Churchill, Gladstone, Disraeli, Macmillan . . . *(Leafs through Piers's script and starts to become interested)* This is jolly radical, the Minister's going to suggest five years compulsory National Service in the Falklands for all young men whose parents earn less than twenty thousand pounds a year . . .

MINISTER *(Fade up)* . . . And therefore we are going to introduce a five-year period of National Service . . .

SIR STEPHEN *(Realisation)* I say, this is an outrage! The entire debate has been written in advance! *(Turns pages)* They've even included the result of the division! We win by 103! What's the point of even turning up!?

Sir Stephen jumps to his feet and waves his order paper. The Labour members make farmyard noises.

SIR STEPHEN *(Heatedly)* Honourable Members, don't you realise what's happening? They're turning Parliament into a music hall! We must . . . *(He is interrupted by a make-up girl who comes and pushes him back into his seat)*

MAKE-UP GIRL You're too bald, the light's bouncing off your forehead . . . *(She dabs glue on his forehead and slaps on a completely mismatched false fringe)* That's better.

SIR STEPHEN How dare you? *(Hand goes to fringe)*

MAKE-GIRL *(Slaps Sir Stephen's wrist)* Leave it alone! It's not dry yet.

SIR STEPHEN I'll report this to the Committee on Privileges!

FLOOR MANAGER *(Typical toughie)* Do you want to be in this show or not, granddad? Because we can always have a by-election and recast!

Sir Stephen looks thoroughly shocked. Then Alan arrives, making a grand entrance across the floor of the House. He wears a gorgeous, new, cream, double-breasted, designer suit, very showbiz. He is also heavily made-up and carefully coiffed. He makes his way along his bench.

ALAN   Out of my way, extras!

Alan makes his way to his place next to Piers, passing the floor manager. They exchange funky hand-slaps and cool words.

FLOOR MANAGER   Main event!

ALAN   Three-ring circus! *(Sits next to Piers)* Piers, are you about to stage a military coup? I don't mind, just give me five minutes to phone my stockbroker.

PIERS   No, I've come straight here from my weekend manoeuvres.

ALAN   So have I, but I washed my face first.

PIERS   My Territorial Army manouevres! We were practising blowing each other up. It was jolly exciting! Only then I got lost, and by the time I was rescued . . .

SIR STEPHEN   I sympathise, Fletcher Dervish. I once got lost on active duty in the Sahara Desert, August 1942, the cruel sun beat remorselessly down . . .

PIERS   I got lost on my way here from Waterloo Station . . .

ALAN   I'm not really interested, Piers. What do you think of the highlights, I've been wrapped in baking foil all morning.

SIR STEPHEN   *(Sudden realisation)* Good God, the man's wearing make-up! I thought we'd seen the last of that sort of thing when Harvey Proctor resigned!

ALAN   It hardly behoves you to criticise, Sir Stephen, what's this, your pet gerbil? *(Rips the false hair from Sir Stephen's forehead. Sir Stephen gives a little cry. Alan smacks the piece onto Piers's chin)* Give us a tune, Acker!

SIR STEPHEN   This is right up your mews, isn't it, B'Stard? This vulgar degradation of a noble tradition!

ALAN *(In a sudden lull in the debate, stands)* I have a dream . . . *(Long pause)* More later. *(Sits)*

PIERS What was it about?

ALAN What?

PIERS Your dream.

ALAN There is no dream. I was lying to attract attention. I'm a politician.

PIERS I get it! *(Stands)* I had a dream too, everybody. I was walking down Oxford Street without my trousers . . . *(Labour shout him down)*

FLOOR MANAGER *(Hurries to Alan)* The Minister's coming to the end of his speech, and the director wants you to go on next.

ALAN *(Mock modest)* Me?!

FLOOR MANAGER You. He adores the suit, the hair, the whole image.

SIR STEPHEN But you can't speak next, B'Stard! The Labour shadow spokesman has to reply to the Minister . . .

FLOOR MANAGER Why?

SIR STEPHEN Why?! Seven hundred years of Parliamentary protocol, that's why!

FLOOR MANAGER Then it's fair dos. Your lot have ballsed up our restrictive practices, so now we're here to balls up yours. Anyway, the Labour spokesman's ugly, stutters and we'd have to relight the whole set . . .

ALAN Don't worry, I'll speak next; I'm not lobby fodder, I have my own heartfelt views, and on such occasions I am prepared to stand up and be counted . . . So what's the debate about?

FLOOR MANAGER Conscription. You're against.

ALAN You got it.

The make-up girl comes over and dabs powder on Alan's chin.

MAKE-UP GIRL Fabulous suit.

ALAN Looks even better over a bedside chair.

MAKE-UP GIRL Your bed or mine?

ALAN *(Banter)* If you're going to play hard to get, forget it . . . *(The girl giggles)*

In wide shot, we see the Minister finish his speech.

MINISTER ... And make Britain a safer place. *(Sits)*

The Labour spokesman stands, but to his immense surprise ...

SPEAKER Alan B'Stard, get on up!

ALAN *(Stands)* Thank you, Mr Speaker, it's a real honour to be here this afternoon, and I mean that sincerely. To the Honourable Members, and to all you wonderful folk watching at home, I just want to say that I oppose conscription with every breath in my perfectly developed body. We don't need to draft our hooligans into the army; there's more than enough vandalism, racism, drunkenness, and mindless violence in the army already. And conscription will take hundreds of thousands of young consumers out of the economy. Young people who are queueing up to buy the latest sound sensation, the Ojuki Personal Compact Disc Jogperson. *(Takes tiny machine from pocket and holds up to camera)* This incredible piece of Japanese high technology which you can ...

MR SPEAKER *(Feels he should interrupt, but he's forgotten his lines. Nerves)* Mr B'Stard! Er ... Prompt ... ?!

FLOOR MANAGER *(Hisses)* Order!

MR SPEAKER *(Shouts)* Order, order!

ALAN Thank you, Mr Speaker ... which you can order by mail from Abbey Stereo, *(Sings)* Call 259 double 6 double 1 ...

Poor Sir Stephen buries his head in his hands, and weeps. The floor manager and the make-up girl are watching Alan on a monitor.

MAKE-UP GIRL He's so televisual!

FLOOR MANAGER A star is born.

2. EXT. HOUSE OF COMMONS. DAY.

A side entrance of the House of Commons. A lot of housewives — Barry Manilow fans, until they saw Alan on TV — are hanging around the door, which is guarded by a policeman. A taxi draws up, Alan gets out and dashes to the door. The women mob him, screaming and scrabbling at his clothes. The policeman rescues him and helps him to the door. There, Alan pauses, picks out a likely looking woman — blonde, buxom, toothy smile — grabs her arm, and whisks her through the door.

3. INT. ALAN'S OFFICE. DAY.

The office looks like the Alan B'Stard fan club headquarters, with piles of merchandising everywhere, and posters of Alan on the wall. Piers, in an 'Alan' T-shirt, is packing various goodies — 'jogpersons' T-shirts, mugs etc. Alan enters, fastening his flies.

ALAN   I hope you've paid for that T-shirt, Piers, that's the last extra large . . . other than what I'm zipping up.

PIERS   Seeing I've been up all night attending to your fan mail, I thought I'd get one for nothing.

ALAN   Well you thought wrong. Twelve pounds ninety-nine please . . . *(Piers pays him)* Have you done my press clippings?

PIERS   *(Sullen)* They're on your desk.

ALAN   *(Picks up a pile of cuttings and flicks through them)* . . . 'The Most charismatic politician since Norman Fowler.' *Daily Telegraph.* I'll assume that's a compliment. 'B'Stard points way to a profit making Parliament.' *Financial Times.* 'Why I'd drop them for Alan B'Stard!' by Jilly Cooper . . . I thought I recognised that housewife!

Sarah enters here with a policeman. He carries a large but not heavy cardboard box. He puts it down and clears off.

SARAH   This arrived for you this morning from Bangkok, and I wasn't going to have it cluttering up the front hall . . .

ALAN   Bangkok! Great! Open it, Piers.

Piers opens the box and extracts a deflated blow-up doll (one of many). Alan takes it and shakes it out. It is an inflatable Alan B'Stard, in a painted on suit, shirt and tie.

SARAH   What the hell is this?

ALAN   An inflatable me. Forty-nine pounds ninety-nine including postage and packing.

SARAH   (*Examines doll. The small valve is where the penis should be*) I see they've made it to scale.

ALAN   It's very cold in Bangkok. Would you like to blow it up, darling?

SARAH   I'd rather drink arsenic.

ALAN   Piers, run down to the chemist, would you?

PIERS   Sorry?

ALAN   (*Gives him the doll*) Just blow this up.

PIERS   What?!

ALAN   Blow it up!

PIERS   If you say so Alan.

Piers opens his desk. It's full of military bits, including some grenades. He removes a grenade, and removes the pin from it.

ALAN   Jesus . . .! (*Dives under desk*)

SARAH   (*Calmly*) I don't think you quite catch Alan's drift, Piers. (*She takes the grenade from Piers and tosses it out of the open window into the Thames. We hear a wet explosion*)

ALAN   (*Coming out from under desk and thrusts doll at Piers*) I meant inflate it, idiot! (*Piers starts blowing up the doll*)

SARAH   (*Watching the doll take shape*) Who on earth is going to buy this obscenity?

ALAN   (*Takes a folder from his desk and empties fifty order forms onto the desk*) So many women, so little time.

SARAH   (*Picks up a few letters and reads one out*) '. . . I'm a lifelong Tory and I think you're the sexiest member around. I have a lovely house in Westminster and another in Dulwich, but all my husband wants to do is play golf and get pissed . . .'

ALAN   (*Snatches the letter*) It isn't . . . ?! (*Realises Sarah has sent him up. He throws the letter down*)

SARAH   You're so vain, Alan. As if She would want to screw you when She's already screwing the whole country!

Piers has now nearly finished blowing up the doll. It looks a bit like Alan. He sits it in Alan's chair to finish blowing it up.

PIERS   Gosh, this is taking forever!
SARAH   It's not that lifelike then.

Piers continues to blow up doll. It looks very rude. Then Sir Stephen enters. He peers myopically at the scene.

SIR STEPHEN   B'Stard, you should know that I've reported you to the ... Good God! Fletcher Dervish, what are you doing? This isn't the Liberal Party!
PIERS   *(Takes mouth from doll)* No, I ...

But the doll now deflates with an uproarious fart.

SIR STEPHEN   If that's going to be the standard of debate in this office, I think I will accept that Peerage ... !

Sir Stephen leaves in a huff. Then the phone rings.

ALAN   Sarah, you answer it. Pretend to be my secretary, it makes an impression ...
SARAH   What's it worth?
ALAN   Oh, for God's sake!

Phone still rings.

SARAH   It won't ring forever. There's a fabulous pair of snakeskin boots ...
ALAN   Have them!
SARAH   ... that I saw in a shop in Tokyo. *(Picks up phone)* Hello, B'Stard Universal Marketing, BUM for short ... *(Sneeringly)* No, I hardly think Mr B'Stard would be interested in appearing in a television game show ...
ALAN   *(Snatches phone, and adopts an American accent)* Hi there ... No, this is his agent ... Just some temporary telephonist. You try to give a dumb kid a start in life and she nearly loses you a million dollar contract ... Sure, Al would adore to appear on *What's The Question?*, if the numbers are right ... Ha ha, that's real funny, I love your limey sense of humour, now let's add some zeros! ... I was thinking ten big ones a show with a twelve appearance guarantee ... It's up to you, but you ain't the only producer in town ... Yeah, we'll be here. *(Hangs up)*

SARAH Do you really think someone's going to pay you ten thousand pounds to appear on some vacuous game show?

PIERS *What's The Question?* isn't vacuous, Sarah, it's really clever! They phone people up, out of the blue, and tell them the answer, and if they can guess the question, they win a prize and get invited to the studio! I watch it every morning, but they've never phoned me.

ALAN Piers, you haven't got a telephone. *(The phone rings again. Alan answers in an American accent)* Hi, Leo Feinstein speaking ... Seven grand a show and fifteen appearances? ... Oh, what the heck, why not, Al's always been a big Nicholas Parsons fan ... Yeah, look forward to it. *(Hangs up. Reverts)* What do you say now, Sarah?

SARAH   I take it all back. Alan B'Stard and a tacky day time TV
programme is a marriage made in heaven — unlike ours.

ALAN   *(Very nasty)* You're just jealous because I'm going to be
the biggest star in Britain! Everyone will know who I am, I'll
be in every paper, and you'll just be a spoilt, anonymous,
middle-class housewife with a shopping fetish. Except when
people see the name on your credit card, they'll say 'are you
related to that brilliant, witty sex warrior who's always on the
telly?' And then they'll want to know all about me!

SARAH   *(Nose to nose with Alan)* Well, if you're very nice to me
— I won't tell them. *(Knees him in the bollocks and makes her
exit)*

4. INT. GAME SHOW STUDIO. DAY.

*Weeks later. A bright, brash game show set, featuring a
ten-foot-high, press button telephone. There are two teams, one
on either side of Nicholas Parsons, the host. Each team consists of
a celeb and a member of the public. One team consists of Roger
Kitter and a boring Yorkshireman. The other team features Alan
and an attractive housewife called Sonia. Cue grams and taped
applause.*

NICHOLAS PARSONS   Hi there phone fans, and we're all
dialling to get hung up on *What's The Question?!!* Our teams
today feature our regular Parliamentary pin-up, Alan 'enormous majority' B'Stard! And what have you been getting
through in Parliament this week, Alan?

ALAN   Two shorthand typists and a canteen lady.

NICHOLAS PARSONS   Faster than directory enquiries! And
Alan's partnering Sonia Ratcliffe, a shop assistant from
Swindon. And we welcome back Roger Kitter, who's just
done a Royal Charity Performance. How did you find the
royals, Rog?

ROGER KITTER   Very friendly, especially Princess Margaret.
If I play my cards right I could have a small part in *Charley's
Aunt.*

NICHOLAS PARSONS Oooh, very naughty for 9.30 on a Thursday morning! And Roger's partner is Harry Fielding from Halifax, who describes himself as 'long-term unemployed'.

ALAN Meaning lazy, ignorant Northerner.

NICHOLAS PARSONS That's the wicked wit we've come to expect from you, Alan.

ALAN Anyone ever told you you're a creep, Nick?

NICHOLAS PARSONS   Everyone. Okay, it's time to ring someone's bell! Everyone press your buttons — now!

*All four contestants bang buttons on their desks, and a number —
0783 34852 — is generated on a display screen on the giant
phone.*

NICHOLAS PARSONS   0783, a Sunderland number . . . Jenny,
bring forth your golden digit!

*Jenny, a busty peroxide blonde in a miniskirt, with one extra
long golden fingernail on her forefinger, comes on to canned
applause. Brandishes her forefinger, then dials this number on a
normal phone, and gives it to Nicholas Parsons. The ringing tone
is heard amplified in the studio.*

NICHOLAS PARSONS   Hope they're not at work . . .
ALAN   You're joking, workshy slob's probably still in bed
sleeping off last night's fifteen pints of Newcastle Brown Ale
. . .

Sonia laughs. Harry looks angry. Roger is really annoyed.

ROGER   Look, Nick, do we have to have this constant, crypto-
Fascist drivel from Alan here? There are a lot of unemployed
people in my industry . . .
ALAN   Yes, this is the first time you've worked for money this
year, isn't it?
ROGER   You unfeeling swine! Where's your Equity card?
You're doing a trade unionist out of work . . . !
ALAN   Three hearty cheers . . . !

*Roger leaves his position and goes for Alan, but Nicholas Parsons
gets between them.*

NICHOLAS PARSONS   All right, all right, that's enough!

A tough, dykie female producer rushes onto the floor.

PRODUCER   Bloody hell, you two! This is supposed to be
mindless fun for the masses, not *Question Time*! Thank Christ
it was only a rehearsal! All right, we'll take a break here . . .

Nick, I've got some notes for you ... *(We close up on producer and Nick)* Firstly, your move on 'Good morning' was too quick, okay?

NICHOLAS PARSONS   Right ...

PRODUCER   And when you introduce the star prize, try to inject a bit more enthusiasm, okay?

NICHOLAS PARSONS   It's hard to wax lyrical over a Russian rust-trap ...

PRODUCER   I know, but we've blown most of the budget on Alan ... *(Looks across to Alan and Sonia's desk, but they've disappeared)* Where is the little prick anyway?

NICHOLAS PARSONS   Anyone seen Al?

ROGER   He's in the Lada with Sonia.

NICHOLAS PARSONS   Not again!

Producer and Nicholas walk around a big paper placard saying 'star prize', and find the Lada, doors open, seats reclining, and Alan and Sonia at it in it.

PRODUCER   I don't want to cramp your style, Al, but it's only a three-minute break.

ALAN   Don't worry, I've finished.

Gets off Sonia, leaving her confused and crumpled in car. He wanders back onto the set, and sees a stage hand lounging about reading the Daily Mirror.

STAGE HAND   'Ere, Al ...

ALAN   Are you addressing me?

STAGE HAND   You just had that Sonia in the back of the Lada?

ALAN   Of course, why?

STAGE HAND   You lucky bugger ...

ALAN   No, we didn't have time for that ...

STAGE HAND   What was it like?

ALAN   Pretty roomy, but the rear suspension's rubbish ...

STAGE HAND   Nice one, Al ... *(Turns the page)* Blimey, look who it isn't! You!

ALAN   You mean it is me or it isn't me?

STAGE HAND   Nah, course it's you. Your missus has written all about you: 'My life of pain with Parliament's kinky TV star by Sarah B'Stard . . .'

Alan snatches the paper. We see a sexy picture of Sarah, and 'Exclusive sizzling serialisation starts on Sunday in The People'.

5. INT. CAR PARK. DAY.

The underground car park of the TV studio. Alan appears. En route to his Bentley, he thumps several cars, starting their alarm systems. The cacophony is deafening. The car park attendant comes from his hut to see what the noise is all about, as Alan drives angrily towards the exit. The attendant has to jump for his life out of Alan's way, as Alan drives straight through the barrier arm, splintering it like balsa wood.

Alan drives off down the road. He stops at some traffic lights. Then he sees a poster on a hoarding. (As big a poster as possible) It's a pic of Alan and Sarah, with a jagged crack between them. The caption says 'My life of pain with Parliament's kinky TV star – coming this Sunday in The People, *the pioneering newspaper'. Alan swears, picks up his car phone and stabs some digits.*

6. INT. ALAN'S LONDON DRAWING ROOM. DAY.

Sarah is rolling about on the hearth rug with two well-formed males, one of them black. The telephone rings and rings. Finally, one of the studs pauses in whatever he's doing, and reaches for the phone and hands it to Sarah.

SARAH   Yes, yes, oh yes!

Intercut between Alan in car, and Sarah on rug.

ALAN   Sarah ... !?
SARAH   *(Controls voice)* Alan? How's the show going?

ALAN　Never mind the show, what the hell do you think you're playing at?!

SARAH　*(Calmly)* What, you mean at this precise moment, darling? *(Hand over receiver)* An inch to the left, Hugo . . . mmm!

ALAN　Everywhere I look I see giant posters advertising your sleazy memoirs!

SARAH　Really?! *(Reacting to Hugo)* Oh, that's fantastic!

ALAN　Fantastic? You selfish bitch, it's an unmitigated disaster! What about my reputation . . . !?

SARAH　I thought you were proud of being an unscrupulous, greedy, evil, sex mad . . .

ALAN　That was before I went into showbiz! *Jackanory* are bound to cancel now!

SARAH　*(Suddenly lets out an ecstatic sigh — this is IT!)* Aaaaaaaaaah!!

ALAN　I think it's a little late for false sympathy, Sarah! *(Throws phone down)*

Sarah and the studs lie in a crumpled heap for a moment. Then . . .

SARAH　Let's have some of his House of Commons champagne. He won't be entitled to it much longer . . .

The black lover, Hugo, pads across to the table where the champagne is cooling, fetches it and glasses, and opens the bottle with a nice pop.

7. EXT. ALAN'S STREET. DAY.

Alan screeches down his Chelsea street, looking for a parking space. There is only one, but a sign shows it is a disabled parking space. Coming the other way is a pale blue invalid car. Alan easily gets the space first. As he parks, the invacar comes alongside and the occupant waves an angry crutch at Alan. But when Alan gets out of his Bentley, he has tucked one leg up under his coat, and hops manically up to his front door.

8. INT. HALL/STAIRS. DAY.

Continuous. Once inside the front door, Alan dashes up the stairs, two at a time. He bursts into the drawing room and finds Sarah and the two men, all dressed, and demurely drinking coffee together. There is no sign that only seconds before, an orgy was taking place.

SARAH Alan! I thought you were phoning from the studio . . .

ALAN Never mind that! Who the hell are these two?!

SARAH This is my agent, Clive . . .

CLIVE *(The white one, adopts a subtly camp pose and a slightly sibilant voice)* Super to meet you, love the make up, it really brings out your cheek bones . . .

ALAN Eugh, a bum-bandit, in my house!

SARAH And Clive's . . . friend, Hugo, my ghost writer.

HUGO *(Not American, but wishes he was)* Real pleasure to meet you, Slim. So you're the dude who dumped Argentinian nuclear waste under a primary school?

ALAN Me!? That's outrageous!

SARAH Yes, but you still did it.

CLIVE Al, I idolise those pictures of you, the tortoise and the peanut butter, they make a sensational spread . . .

ALAN All right, Sarah, this has gone far enough. As your husband, I order you to evict these 'Clause Twenty-Eighters' and withdraw your article from Sunday's paper, or I'll blow torch all your credit cards!

SARAH Fire away, darling, they're paying me a hundred thousand pounds, and I've already had quite a lot up front!

ALAN A hundred thousand?!

CLIVE It is a six-week serialisation.

SARAH And we're negotiating the UK and US book rights, the mini-series starring Joan Collins . . .

ALAN Yes, that's about right, you portrayed by a fifty-year-old Polyfilla advert . . .

SARAH No, she wants to play you, Alan. And I'm on *Wogan* next Monday . . .

ALAN Huh, big deal. Anyone can get on *Wogan*!

SARAH Who's talking about the programme?

9. EXT. 10 DOWNING STREET. NIGHT.

We should construct the most famous front door in the world in the studio. There's a middle-aged copper on duty. Big Ben is sounding eleven. Alan rushes up to the door.

POLICEMAN   Excuse me sir, where do you think you're going? This is 10 Downing Street, you know . . .

ALAN   Is it really? Fancy not knowing that, and me a Member of Parliament. I must nearly be stupid enough to be a policeman.

POLICEMAN   *(Recognises the style)* I know that acerbic wit! You're Alan . . . Alan . . . Alan Thing, aren't you?! I've seen you on that what's it called, thingy, I watch it every day. Oh dear . . . er . . .

ALAN   *What's The Question?*

POLICEMAN   That's the one! Never miss it, blinding show!

ALAN   Yes, it is very popular with the educationally sub-normal. Now, I must see the Prime . . .

POLICEMAN   What's he like then, you know, er, wotsisface, tall bloke, very smooth, blazer, crinkly hair, butter-wouldn't-melt type, women love him, you know . . .

ALAN   Cecil Parkinson?

POLICEMAN   That's right, Nicholas Parsons! The wife adores him, but he's a bit too oily for my liking, I'm more your Ted . . . you know, wotsisface, bloke with the twitchy hand and the dustbin . . . I nicked him once, real sport . . . Here, test me.

ALAN   What are you talking . . . ?!

POLICEMAN   I'm as clever as the berks you get on your show. Go on, tell me an answer, go on, like you was phoning me up at home, and I'll guess the question, go on.

ALAN   *(Seething)* In five seconds I'm going to take your truncheon and ram it right up your . . .

POLICEMAN   Got it! 'What will you do to me if I don't let you see the PM?'

ALAN   Correct.

POLICEMAN   I love quizzes. I can't make any promises, but seeing you're Alan Thingie, I'll cop a blind-un . . . Go on, knock her up.

Copper moves out of view, and Alan raps on the door. No reply.
He knocks again. Then there's a voice from behind the door.

MRS THATCHER *(Loud whisper)* Cecil! I thought I told you to use the back entrance?!

ALAN *(Calls through door)* No, it's me, Alan B'Stard, a lowly but loyal backbencher on a mission of national security . . .

The door opens, and standing there, almost unrecognisable in curlers and face pack and dressing gown, is SHE.

MRS THATCHER Come in, you little turd, I've been expecting you.

10. INT. PM'S STUDY. NIGHT.

The study is small, over-furnished, book-lined and intimidating. The walls and carpet are red, a fire flickers in the grate, it's all a little like hell. Mrs Thatcher sits behind her desk, Alan kneels in front of it.

ALAN . . . Sarah claims she's been intimate with half of your ministers − presumably the bottom half, and they've told her everything! She reveals the truth about the Belgrano, your part in the Westland scandal, how much Nigel Lawson has in his Swiss Bank Account, the real reason Jeffrey Archer gave Monica Coghlan two thousand pounds, the date and result of the next General Election, and why Rhodes Boyson has that ridiculous hair cut! The Party will never recover . . .

MRS THATCHER Balls! You're just trying to save your own pimply, perfumed neck! Well let me tell you, B'Stard, the Conservative Party is bigger than one over-sexed little member! Since I've been Leader we've survived pederasts, sanctions-busters, swindlers, slum landlords and bigamists, and that's just in the Cabinet. But I still win and keep on winning! So why should I stop Robert Maxwell publishing? More power to his elbow say I − if he can find it under all that fat!

ALAN But I'll be ruined!

MRS THATCHER   That's why I instructed your wife to write her autobiography. *(Alan is amazed)* Did you really think I would let you get away with turning the Commons into a tawdry advertising medium – and upstaging me?!

ALAN   I was only trying to be true to the spirit of Thatcherism . . .

MRS THATCHER   Bullshit! All you care about is number one!

ALAN   I thought that's what Thatcherism was all about?

MRS THATCHER   Of course it is, but we can't let the common herd know that, they have to believe the Conservative Party stands for God and a strong pound, not greed and an untraceable Deutschmark account in the Cayman Islands. You can resign now if you want to, and save yourself the postage; though I think suicide would be the shrewder political option. Now get out! *(Crosses to the door, and opens it for Alan. Suddenly they hear the sound of someone falling down the stairs)* Oh for God's sake, Denis, go back to bed!

11. INT. ALAN'S OFFICE. NIGHT.

Alan's office, dark. The sound of snoring. Piers can dimly be seen sleeping on the chaise longue. He wears striped flannel pyjamas, and cuddles an old teddy bear. Alan enters and puts on the light. The room is still full of fan club merchandise.

ALAN   Piers! What are you doing? No, that's a silly question, you're sleeping. But why here?

PIERS   You told me not to leave until I'd sent out all these 'B'Stard Sings the Blues' albums . . .

ALAN   But I looked in a little while ago . . .

PIERS   Well . . . I had to go to the toilet once.

ALAN   No?! That must have been the precise moment I poked my head round the door. Gosh, your luck's really out, and it's so unfair! You're so loyal, yet people are saying these terrible things about you . . .

PIERS   What are they saying, Alan?

ALAN   There's a vicious story about the PM's private life in next Sunday's *People*! All lies, of course – well mostly – but you know how mud sticks! And the awful thing is, the story can only have been written by a Tory MP! The entire Parliamentary Party has been crammed into committee room A all evening, trying to identify the traitor! Every one of us had to swear on the Bible – except for Michael Heseltine, who swore on a copy of his autobiography – that we knew nothing about this vicious libel on the greatest Prime Minister in history! Only one member didn't take the oath. Can you guess who?

PIERS   That's easy, the Prime Minister.

ALAN   No, YOU, Piers! Now everyone believes you're the renegade! They're laying odds you'll be giving a press conference in Moscow on Monday.

PIERS   Oh my God, I can't even speak Russian!

ALAN   I blame myself. I should have realised you'd be toiling here, loyal, faithful . . . stupid . . .

PIERS   What can I do, Alan? Help me!

ALAN   How? The newspaper comes out the day after tomorrow . . . *(Smacks fist into palm)* God, I hate the gutter press, with their lurid pin-ups, their nasty, common adverts for the Co-op and Pontins, and their wicked sensationalistic lies! I hate the way they blow up innocent stories, blow them up out of all proportion, and blow up innocent lives . . . !

PIERS   Alan, I've got it! I'll get up very, very early on Sunday morning, and buy all the copies of *The People* before anyone can read them!

ALAN   Piers, that's brilliant. Cost a bit, of course: say two million copies at twenty-five pence, but on the plus side, you'd win the bingo . . .

PIERS   You're right, it wouldn't work. Where would I find time to fill in two million bingo coupons? *(Starts getting tearful and cries)* Oh, Alan, you must help me, I'll do anything to prove my loyalty to Her! *(Drapes himself over Alan)*

ALAN   *(Pushing Piers off like a stick insect)* For God's sake Piers, stop blubbing! I thought you were a brave resourceful Territorial Army Officer?

PIERS   Only on weekends, Alan, when I put my uniform on.

ALAN   But it is the weekend, Piers. And your uniform's hanging behind that door . . .

12. EXT. PRINT WORKS. NIGHT.

Dark, quiet. The sound of the Thames lapping nearby. A torch switches on, and illuminates a sign. The sign reads 'Mirror Newspapers – Docklands Print Centre'. Then we see a gloved hand wind wires around the terminals of a plunger style detonator. The hand presses the plunger down. Nothing happens. The hand unwinds the wires and reverses them, then pushes the plunger again. There is a huge explosion as the print works goes up in flames. Sound of dogs barking and alarm bells ringing.

13. INT. COMMONS CHAMBER. NIGHT.

Alan is on his feet in an almost empty House, making a speech.
He has several flashes sewn to his suit, tennis player style.

ALAN ... And the awful news we have just heard, of the terrible explosion and fire at the new Sunday *People* printworks, only underlines the importance of compulsory fire prevention equipment, as proposed by my amendment. And in my opinion and that of countless experts, the best fire prevention equipment is supplied by Checkland and Birt, the Distinguished Extinguishers, who've been damping things down since 1987. *(Produces a small fire extinguisher, car size)* Call Freefone 345 and just shout 'Fire!'

Piers enters, panting, in his battle fatigues. His face is scorched, and his jacket smoulders lightly. He approaches Alan, beams and gives the thumbs up. Alan sprays his smouldering jacket with foam ...

The Haltemprice Bunker

1. INT. ALAN'S OFFICE. DAY.

Alan, in his shirtsleeves, is standing in front of a mirror, trimming his nasal hair with some nail scissors. Piers is at his desk, watching.

ALAN ... So there's the Chancellor of the Exchequer speechifying about how a huge balance of payments deficit is a sign of a booming economy, and the TV cameras are pointing right up the hairiest snout outside London Zoo. Well, now the ordinaries can see their masters on the small screen, the age of the fat slob in the crumpled suit is over! Move over, Nigel, and let Mr Sex balance the Budget!

At this point Pickles, an old messenger, arrives with mail.

PICKLES Morning, young masters ... *(Puts a pile of letters on Alan's desk, and hands a single piece of mail to Piers, who considers it sadly)*

ALAN Anything interesting, Pickles?

PICKLES Just the usual constituency junk mail, sir. Shall I lose them for you?

ALAN Yes, but steam the stamps off the s.a.e.'s first. *(Pickles*

takes Alan's mail and exits)

PIERS *(Appalled)* Alan, you can't do that, we're here to serve our constituents! At least, I am.

ALAN Really? Then how ironic that Yassar Arafat gets more Jewish New Year cards than you get constituents' letters.

PIERS Does he? *(Opens his letter. He is elated, he waves his letter at Alan)* I've got it, I've got it!

ALAN What's that, a letter from the clap clinic?

PIERS No, my Gold Credit Card! *(The card is attached to the letter. Piers looks at it lovingly)* The one you proposed me for! Thank you, thank you, I didn't think I'd be glamorous enough, not for a gold card. Does that mean I'm a Yuppie at last?

ALAN It certainly does, Piers, just as everyone else was packing it in. Still, this calls for a celebratory lunch. We'll have to go somewhere expensive though, they don't take Gold Cards at cheap joints like the House of Commons dining room.

PIERS *(Excited)* I can pay?

ALAN *(Smiles graciously)* Of course: a credit card is like a dick, if you don't use it every day, it withers away.

PIERS What's a dick, Alan?

ALAN You are, Piers.

PIERS Better use me every day then, Alan!

ALAN No, I meant . . . oh, never mind! *(They exit)*

2. EXT. PARLIAMENT SIDE GATE. DAY.

There is a mass lobby of the Commons in progress, and a line of respectable looking protesters snakes past a side gate of Parliament, where an armed policeman stands on duty. The protesters carry banners bearing such slogans as

'Bring war criminals to justice'
'Prosecute known Nazis living in Britain'
'Never forgive, never forget'

Alan and Piers come out of the side gate, and a few protesters gather round them.

ALAN Stand back, scum, MP coming through!

FEMALE PROTESTER Mr B'Stard, you must sign our petition!

ALAN How much will you pay me?

FEMALE PROTESTER Nothing, of course.

ALAN Then piss off!

FEMALE PROTESTER But there are Nazi war criminals living free, as British citizens! *(Pushes leaflets at Alan and Piers)*

ALAN Who cares? *(Drops leaflet, but Piers pockets his. Alan turns to cop)* Officer, aren't these people causing an obstruction? Disperse them, use your gun if necessary. *(Strides off)*

FEMALE PROTESTER *(Shouts after Alan)* You'd have loved it under Hitler, wouldn't you?

ALAN *(Shouts back over his shoulder)* Eva Braun had no complaints!

A few feet away, an old woman hails a passing taxi. It stops, she makes to get in, but Alan knocks her out of the way, and gets into cab. Piers scuttles over and joins him, smiling sheepishly at furious old lady.

3. INT. MUSSOLINI'S. DAY.

Mussolini's is a seriously trendy Italian restaurant, decorated in black, grey, and white, with lots of spotlights, and fashionable, uncomfortable dining chairs around black ash tables. There are pictures of Benito Mussolini on the wall, and the waiters wear black shirts. The place is full of business people. Some are the dreaded Yuppies, eating warm chicken liver salad and comparing filofaxes. Others are fat, middle-aged business persons pigging out. Alan and Piers are shown to a round table where a tall young man already sits. He is Piers Lonsdale, a financial journalist. Alan and Piers sit, Alan next to Piers Lonsdale. A waiter — a perfectly ordinary middle-aged man — gives each a starkly modernist menu and a rather half-hearted fascist salute.

PIERS LONSDALE *(Half rises and shakes Alan's hand)* Alan, stupendous to see you. How's the old portfolio?

ALAN Getting fatter, thanks to your Rowntree's tip . . .

PIERS LONSDALE My pleasure, and thank you for the Budget leak.

ALAN No problem. I enjoyed getting it out of Nigel's secretary nearly as much as I enjoyed putting it in first. Now, Piers . . .

PIERS LONSDALE Yes?

PIERS Yes?

PIERS LONSDALE Ah, so we have two Piers?

PIERS Like Brighton. *(Giggles)*

PIERS LONSDALE *(Coldly to Piers)* I don't think I know you . . .

ALAN Piers Lonsdale, financial journalist of the year; Piers Fletcher Dervish, here solely to pay for lunch.

PIERS LONSDALE *(Shakes Piers's hand briefly)* No disrespect to your pet, Alan, but I thought this was to be a discreet insider dealing session?

ALAN Don't worry, our conversation will be rather like Burt Reynolds's toupee . . . considerably above his head.

Alan and Piers Lonsdale exchange smiles. Piers Lonsdale quite understands Piers Fletcher Dervish's function. Then the waiter returns.

WAITER Are you ready to order now, gentlemen?

PIERS LONSDALE Good God, you're ugly!

WAITER *(Taken aback)* I beg your pardon, sir?

PIERS LONSDALE Ugly and deaf, Alan.

ALAN *(Very loudly and clearly)* Go away and send us a presentable waiter without handicap.

The waiter gives a long-suffering half smile, and takes a couple of steps back, and . . . waits.

PIERS Don't you think that was rather rude, Piers?

PIERS LONSDALE Rude Piers? But he's a servant, you can't not be rude to a servant, can you, Alan?

ALAN   Course not, only language they understand.

PIERS LONSDALE   Do you think so? But this is supposed to be an Italian restaurant. *(Raises voice)* Guiseppe, avanti!

WAITER   Yes, sir?

ALAN   I thought we asked for a better looking waiter ... *(Wrinkles nose)* And one without body odour!

WAITER   It's not body odour, sir. I wear a clove of garlic around my neck to ward off vampires.

PIERS   Really, does it work?

WAITER   Apparently not sir.

PIERS LONSDALE   Cheeky wop!

WAITER   *(Doggedly)* Shall I tell you about today's specials?

ALAN   No, just translate something for us.

WAITER   What sir?

ALAN   The entire menu.

WAITER   Very well sir.

PIERS LONSDALE   Into Russian . . .

WAITER   I'm afraid I can't do that, sir.

ALAN   Not much of a restaurant, is it?

PIERS LONSDALE   I suppose you can translate it into English?

WAITER   Of course sir.

PIERS LONSDALE   Then pray do so.

WAITER   Gamberetti are prawns, which we grill with . . .

ALAN   Sing it.

WAITER   I beg your pardon?

ALAN   Hearing's no better then?

PIERS   *(Embarrassed, to waiter)* Just his little joke.

PIERS LONSDALE   I thought he was just here to pay?

ALAN   That's right. Be quiet, Piers, haven't you got anything to read?

A crushed Piers takes from his pocket the leaflet the demonstrator gave him, and starts to read.

WAITER   Would you like to see the wine list?

PIERS LONSDALE   You were asked to sing the menu, Pavarotti!

ALAN   To the tune of 'Volare'.

WAITER   I don't think I know that song.

ALAN   I'll start you off. *(Sings)* Prawn cocktail, oh oh
Chef's pate, oh oh oh oh.
Fish soup, ne blinkedy bloop . . .

WAITER   And to follow, sir?

PIERS LONSDALE   *(Tetchy)* Stop trying to be witty and fetch us a bottle of the most expensive wine in the house.

Waiter goes off.

PIERS   *(Looks up from leaflet)* This is the most amazing thing, Alan! Apparently, in the last war, we were on the same side as the Russians! Do you think someone should tell Mrs Thatcher?

Piers Lonsdale and Alan completely ignore Piers.

ALAN   So fill me in on that little Chilean investment opportunity . . .

PIERS LONSDALE   Yes, absolutely. *(With a sweep of his arm,
Piers Lonsdale clears the table of flowers, bread, cruets, cutlery, and
wine glasses. All the nearby diners turn and look, some of them
laugh. Then he gets his portable computer from under the table, and
puts it in front of him and Alan. He switches on and flips up the
screen)* Now, as you know, Chilean mining shares have
boomed since General Pinochet introduced slave labour . . .
(Presses some more buttons) so I've set up an investment fund,
the Santiago High Income Trust . . .

ALAN   S.H.I.T. . . ?!

PIERS LONSDALE   Yes, an unfortunate oversight, but we've
done all the paperwork now, so we're stuck with it . . .

The waiter comes back with a dusty bottle of fine claret.

WAITER   The finest bottle we have, a 1945 Château Mouton
Rothschild, with a hand-painted label by Salvador Dali.
*(Offers the bottle to Alan for him to inspect the label. Alan blows the
dust off the bottle into waiter's face. Waiter manages, just, not to
sneeze. He uncorks the bottle reverently)* This is believed to be the
only bottle of this great vintage left in Britain. *(Gives Piers
Lonsdale the cork to sniff)*

PIERS LONSDALE   You'd better try it, Alan. My taste buds
aren't firing on all cylinders; Frank Bough warned me five
grams of coke a day might have that effect.

*Piers Lonsdale passes cork to Alan, who sniffs it, shrugs, and
passes it to Piers, who's still immersed in leaflet. He tries to eat
the cork.*

PIERS   Eugh, don't like these canapés much, Alan.

ALAN   *(To Piers Lonsdale)* Inbred, Piers.

PIERS   Oh, right. *(Takes a piece of bread from the bread basket,
puts the cork on it, and takes a brave bite, chews and swallows –
with difficulty)*

PIERS LONSDALE   *(To waiter)* We haven't all day, Luigi. Pour
a slug. *(The waiter carefully pours a taster. Piers Lonsdale sniffs,*

swirls, tastes and spits into the pouch in the waiter's pinny) It's disgusting.

WAITER That's impossible!

PIERS LONSDALE Don't argue with me, you cheeky Eyetie! I own a petit château in the Medoc! I don't suppose you own two pairs of shoes! Bring another bottle . . .

WAITER But this was the last . . .

ALAN Then throw it away and bring some mineral water . . .

WAITER Throw it away? It cost nine hundred and fifty pounds!

PIERS LONSDALE *(Knocks bottle from waiter's hands. It smashes on the tiled floor)* Oh dear, you've dropped it, so that's all academic now, isn't it?

ALAN *(Points to floor)* And clear up that mess, this is West One, not West Beirut!

Waiter goes off muttering.

PIERS LONSDALE Now, where were we?

ALAN S.H.I. . .

PIERS LONSDALE Ah, yes. I'll be endorsing the fund in my many newspaper columns and on my award-winning television programme, so everyone will want a piece of . . . er . . . but as you're an old friend, I've reserved you half a million's worth . . .

ALAN That's very white of you, but money's a little tight just now, what with it being Thursday. I can only lay my hands on a hundred thou of liquid cash . . .

PIERS LONSDALE Is that all? Oh well, better than nothing, I suppose . . .

PIERS But Alan, you mustn't invest in Chile! The Prime Minister said so only last week in the House!

PIERS LONSDALE I know. Odd, really, because yesterday, her P.P.S. bought half a million pounds worth of . . .

ALAN Number twos?

PIERS LONSDALE Quite.

The waiter returns with dustpan and brush, mop, and bin liner to clean up floor.

PIERS Alan, it says here there are hundreds of Nazi murderers working and living in Chile . . . !

ALAN Of course. That's probably why the slave labour brigades are so efficiently run.

PIERS LONSDALE Spot on . . . Why is your homunculus so obsessed with Nazis? What's he reading?

PIERS It's a real eye-opener, Piers, it's awful! Did you know Hitler even tried to invade England?

PIERS LONSDALE Well I never. Excuse me . . . *(Takes leaflet from Piers)*

ALAN It's litter, thrust on us by a bunch of ordinaries, cluttering up the pavement outside the House . . .

PIERS LONSDALE *(Glancing at leaflet)* Are there really Nazi fugitives living in Britain?

ALAN Maybe. Who knows, who cares . . .

PIERS LONSDALE I think you're missing a trick here, Alan. Of course *we* don't care, but take my word as an award-winning scribe, for an MP to unmask a Nazi would have fantastic spin-off, publicity-wise, politics-wise, and profit-wise.

ALAN Profit-wise?

PIERS LONSDALE Of course. There are more Jews in the Cabinet than on the board of Marks and Sparks. Play your cards right on this one and you could have a ministerial car and free chicken Kievs for life.

ALAN I like it! *(Turns on Piers)* You're supposed to be my friend, why didn't you think of that, oaf!?

PIERS What do you mean?

ALAN How many times have I told you? Everything a politician does can be exploited for personal advantage! Your problem − well, one of many − is that you never show any initiative! Can I borrow your phone, Piers?

Piers Lonsdale takes a small Cellnet from a pocket and hands it to Alan, who taps some keys.

ALAN Hello, BBC? Alan B'Stard MP here, biggest majority in the House of Commons, put me through to the producer of

World at One . . . (Beat) Just calling to confirm my interview on tomorrow's show . . . Then rearrange your precious schedule, Edwina can go on *Woman's Hour!* Don't start bleating about editorial independence or I'll put Lord Rees of Mogg onto you . . . ! That's better. *(Cuts off)* Now I'm hungry! Gianfranco, mangare! *(Points at open mouth)*

WAITER Oh . . . *(Puts down mop, and gets out pen and pad)* Yes sir?

ALAN We want food.

WAITER I know, I'm waiting to take your order . . . sir.

ALAN Order? You're the nit-picking, Neopolitan know-it-all, empathise. Bring what you think we'd like.

The waiter, seething now, turns to hors d'oeuvres trolley, gets three plates and slaps all sorts of things on them, and plonks them down in front of the three diners.

PIERS Oh, that looks super! *(Tucks napkin into collar in anticipation)*

ALAN We didn't order this muck!

WAITER You didn't actually order anything!

ALAN Don't take that tone of voice with me, Benito!

PIERS LONSDALE Your attitude has been surly and sarcastic from the start. Get the manager.

PIERS *(Wistfully looking at waiter's tray)* Can't I just have a nibble . . . ?

The manager has heard the raised voices, and hurries over.

MANAGER What seems to be the matter?

ALAN The matter, Guido, is this waiter.

PIERS LONSDALE Sack him.

MANAGER But why?

ALAN Because he's made sexual advances to Piers Fletcher Dervish MP, here.

PIERS What?!

PIERS LONSDALE And because we're very, very rich, and if you don't dismiss him, we'll stop coming here, and so will all our friends.

The manager sadly shrugs his shoulders at waiter, who bangs his tray down on the table and storms out of the restaurant.

PIERS LONSDALE *(Looks at watch)* Well, I'd better be toddling, I'm so important I've got another lunch next door.

ALAN Yes, I'd better make a move too, Fergie's old man's putting me up for his club this afternoon . . .

Alan and Piers Lonsdale leave the restaurant. The manager goes to remove the three starters.

PIERS *(To manager)* Oh, no, leave them, please . . . *(The manager leaves the plates in front of Piers, who tucks in)*

4. EXT. RESTAURANT. DAY.

(In the studio) Alan and Piers Lonsdale exit the caff. A one-legged beggar is propped against the wall, an army beret outstretched for charity.

BEGGAR *(Holds out beret)* Remember the Falklands, Captain?

ALAN Indeed I do, I made a fortune!

He and Piers Lonsdale move off, chortling. Suddenly, the sacked waiter, screaming like a samurai, comes charging towards them, a large Sabatier knife in his hand. Alan cowers, but Piers Lonsdale disposes of the waiter with a single karate chop.

PIERS LONSDALE *(To a startled looking Alan)* It happens all the time.

5. INT. RADIO STUDIO. DAY.

The next day, inside a small, shabby BBC radio studio. Alan sits opposite an attractive lady interviewer – preferably Anna Ford – across a table. A big mike hangs down, and both Alan and Anna wear cans. Throughout the interview, Alan is surreptitiously trying to look down the front of 'Anna's' blouse.

ALAN   ... A mission in life, Anna. To bring these evil Nazi animals to justice, wherever they may be hiding.

ANNA   And how many Nazi war criminals are there actually living in Britain?

ALAN   Oh ... *(Not prepared)* Lots.

ANNA   Can you name any of them?

ALAN   Well ... there's bound to be at least one called Fritz, isn't there? *(Laughs. She doesn't)*

ANNA   And the Home Secretary is supporting you?

ALAN   Is he? Oh, that's good to hear ...

ANNA   No, it was a rhetorical question, Mr B'Stard, isn't your whole crusade simply a publicity stunt?

ALAN   Anna, do I need publicity? I'm young, handsome, virile, I have the largest majority you're ever likely to see, I attract a crowd just going to the shop for a packet of Mates ...

ANNA   *(Cuts in)* Alan B'Stard, thank you. *(Takes off cans)*

ALAN   Thank you, Anna. *(Takes off his cans)* I thought that went rather well.

ANNA   Did you? I thought you were awful. Unprepared, unprofessional, unpersuasive ...

ALAN *(Unfazed)* But an unbelievably brilliant lover.

ANNA What?!

ALAN I'll prove it to you. There's a nice little hotel around the corner that all the BBC big nobs use, books rooms out by the hour . . .

ANNA But what would we do with the other fifty-nine minutes? Watch *Santa Barbara*?

ALAN Who's been talking?!

ANNA When I announced you were coming on the programme, your wife phoned me . . .

ALAN Interfering bitch! *(Anna gathers her things and heads for the door. Alan bars her way and makes her squeeze past)* Look at it this way, Anna, with a man as hot as me, a minute is all a woman can take before she bursts into flames. Come on . . .

ANNA Mr B'Stard, I wouldn't do it with you if the human race had been annihilated by a thermo-nuclear exchange, we were the only two survivors, and the future of mankind depended on our coupling. *(Pushes past him and exits)*

ALAN Is that a 'no'?

6. EXT. HALTEMPRICE SUBURB. DAY.

Alan's Bentley drives down an anonymous row of neat, semi-detached houses. We hear a recording Alan has made of his interview with Anna.

ALAN 'I want the world to know that no filthy Nazi can sleep secure in his bed now that I, Alan B'Stard, am on his trail.'

Alan pulls up and parks outside one particular house, and walks up to the front door. He hammers on the door, Gestapo style. The door is opened by a wizened little man in his middle seventies.

ALAN Bad news Helmut, you old Nazi, I'm going to have to turn you in.

7. INT. NAZI'S HOUSE. DAY.

The front room of Helmut Drucker's house. It is a typical 'Between the Wars' semi, but furnished Munich 1935: heavy Gothic furniture, Nazi memorabilia on the walls, a large, framed picture of Hitler in pride of place, with a smaller picture of Margaret Thatcher nearby. A tailor's dummy in a corner models Drucker's SS tunic and peaked cap. Alan sits in a comfy chair while Drucker faces the room — has he got a wooden leg? — agitatedly.

HELMUT DRUCKER   ... You can not have me arrested, it would be the end of everything! It would mean life imprisonment, at least!

ALAN   You should have thought of that before you did those naughty things.

HELMUT DRUCKER   But it's not fair!

ALAN   Helmut, you know it's not in my nature to moralise, but you did murder fifty thousand civilians!

HELMUT DRUCKER   They were only Croatians! Sub-human Slavs! Haven't you read *Mein Kampf*!?

ALAN   No, Norman Tebbit hasn't returned it to the House of Commons library.

HELMUT DRUCKER   Then let me tell you, the Führer was right! I did my duty, and I'm not ashamed that I wore the Fuhrer's uniform!

ALAN   Did you? Then what did the Führer wear, Eva Braun's frock?

HELMUT DRUCKER   *(Ranting now)* The Führer never wore women's clothes! That was a vicious rumour put around by Stalin. Silk underwear perhaps, but frocks, never never never!

Spittle flies from Drucker's lips, as his dentures are loose. Alan takes his hankie out and mops face.

ALAN   I suppose he didn't have the legs for it.

Drucker angrily slaps Alan. Alan punches him in the stomach. The old man subsides into his chair, wheezing.

HELMUT DRUCKER   It's all so unjust! I'm a fugitive in the tripe-eating capital of Europe, and Kurt Waldheim is President of Austria! And it wasn't fifty thousand civilians, it was thirty-seven thousand, tops!

ALAN   That hardly constitutes a plea for clemency, does it? You're still guilty of hideous offences against humanity.

HELMUT DRUCKER   So? Haven't I paid for my crime? Isn't the thousand pounds a month I've been giving you enough anymore?! When you started blackmailing me, you never said that it was going to be index-linked! ... So how much do you want now? Fifteen hundred? Two thousand?

ALAN   Helmut, my disgusting old Obersturmbannführer, when I started blackmailing you, a thousand a month was serious money to me. But now that business is booming, you're worth more to me in the dock of outraged public opinion.

HELMUT DRUCKER   And I thought we were friends! What about the political advice I've given you ... ?

ALAN   What, burn down Parliament and blame it on the socialists? Very sophisticated!

HELMUT DRUCKER   It worked for us in 1933!

ALAN   Britain today is not the same as Germany under Hitler!

HELMUT DRUCKER   No, in Germany, the newspapers were more independent.

ALAN   Rubbish! And I haven't come here for a history lesson, I've come to turn you in. Millions of people and Anna Ford are depending on me. May I use your telephone?

HELMUT DRUCKER   Nein, nein, nein ... ! *(Tries to stop Alan, but he pushes the old man back into his chair and picks up the phone)*

ALAN   Helmut, you're psychic. *(Dials)* Nine ...

HELMUT DRUCKER   Five thousand pounds a month?

ALAN   Mmmm ... I won't deny it's tempting ... *(Dials)* Nine ...

HELMUT DRUCKER   Ten thousand pounds?

ALAN   *(Hesitates)* If only I weren't so rich already ... *(Dials)* Nine. Police, please ... Hello, Alan B'Stard MP here. You may have heard me launch my anti-Nazi crusade on *The World at One* . . . Well, I'm delighted to be able to tell you . . .

HELMUT DRUCKER *(Flings open the door of a sideboard, to reveal . . .)* All right, half a million in Nazi gold!

ALAN *(Eyes pop out)* . . . that if I find any Nazis around here, you'll be the first to hear.

8. EXT. SHOPPING STREET. DAY.

Piers walks into frame, obviously running an errand, we hear Alan's voice over.

ALAN *(V/O)* . . . The ticket's for an extremely old constituent who is, alas, dying of a not very photogenic disease. His only brother lives in Chile, so I'm arranging this touching little reunion. I want you to go to the travel agent . . . *(Piers wanders into a public convenience)* No, the travel agent . . . *(Piers comes out of the toilet and goes into a nearby travel agency)* And book a one way ticket to Antofagasta, Chile . . .

9. INT. TRAVEL AGENT. DAY.

(Could be done on location?) Piers is at the desk, being served by a competent black clerk.

CLERK . . . You'll have to change at Madrid, and Santiago, is that okay?

(ALAN *(V/O)* And don't answer any questions!

PIERS I'm sorry, I can't say.

CLERK *(Puzzled)* Suit yourself . . . Smoking or non smoking? *(But Piers's lips remain resolutely closed)* Is there anything you'd like to ask me?

(ALAN *(V/O)* And don't ASK any questions either!

So Piers shakes his head dumbly at clerk.

CLERK *(Becoming hostile)* Would you rather be served by a white person?!

Piers wants to deny this, but is afraid to speak, so he agonises for a moment, then picks up the travel documents and rushes out of the shop.

10. INT. ALAN'S OFFICE. DAY.

Alan is on the phone.

ALAN   ... So it looks as if I'll be able to take the whole half million pounds worth of S.H.I.T. after all ... *(Piers Fletcher Dervish enters)* See you tomorrow then, Piers. *(Hangs up)*

PIERS   What? Oh, right ... *(Turns to go)*

ALAN   Not you, dunce. Well, have you got them? Give, give! *(Piers hands over a wallet of travel documents, which Alan examines)*

PIERS   You did say you'd reimburse me, didn't you Alan? Only I did pay on my credit card ...

ALAN   Of course I'll reimburse you, if you're that obsessed with petty cash ...

PIERS   It was over two thousand pounds!

ALAN   Exactly; petty ... *(Spots error with ticket)* Why is this ticket in your name!? I told you it was for Helmut Drucker!

PIERS   But you said not to answer any questions, so when the clerk asked who the ticket was for ...

ALAN   God! Go back to the travel agent, and get them to change the name ...

PIERS   *(Sulky)* Only if you ask me nicely.

ALAN   *(Threatening)* What?!

PIERS   Ask me nicely. I'm fed up with you always being so beastly to me! I'm a person too!

ALAN   Then prove it! Show some initiative.

PIERS   All right, I will! *(Marches out. Beat. Marches back, sheepishly)* Forgot the tickets.

11. EXT. HALTEMPRICE STATION. DAY.

A small branch line station, old fashioned, now part of an enthusiasts'-run steam railway, such as the North York Moors railway. Very early morning, and quite misty. Suitable edgy guitar music. In the distance we see Alan's Bentley driving towards the station. The Bentley arrives, and Alan gets out. He wears a cashmere coat and black leather gloves. There is no-one else around. He waits. After a few moments, an old Mercedes drives up, Drucker at the wheel. It stops boot to boot with the Bentley. Drucker gets out. He wears a black, leather trenchcoat and a soft, felt hat. And unlocks his boot. It holds a dozen gold bars. Alan unlocks his boot, and indicates the old boy should transfer the gold without Alan's help. Drucker does so, painfully. Alan shuts his boot, and leads Drucker past the unmanned ticket barrier.

12. EXT. PLATFORM. DAY.

The platform is deserted and desolate. The opposite platform seems empty too. It features an old waiting room. Alan and Drucker wait for the train. Alan removes his gloves and puts them in a pocket. He takes a travel agent's folder from his pocket and gives it to Drucker, who extracts the rail ticket.

HELMUT DRUCKER *(Looking at the rail ticket)* Second class?

ALAN I'm sorry, a Herr Himmler had reserved the cattle truck.

Suddenly, a mob of journalists, photographers and TV crews emerge from the waiting room, with Piers at their head. Alan and Drucker are stunned.

PIERS No initiative, eh, Alan? I think you'll find you were wrong about me!

The cameras whirr and click.

HELMUT DRUCKER *(To Alan, viciously)* Sie Gemeiner Schweinehund Dafur Werden Sie Bussen Sie Mistvieh!

ALAN *(Wipes face)* That's easy for you to say!

HELMUT DRUCKER You've set me up! *(Grabs Alan's lapels)*

ALAN   *(Wrenching Drucker's hands away)* No, no, why would I?

HELMUT DRUCKER   *(Fierce whisper)* Because you're obsessed
   with money and power, I've seen it all before, you idiot
   ... Well, when the police get here, I'll tell them how you've
   blackmailed me all these years. *(Starts to shout)* I'm not
   ashamed of what I did, not ashamed of what we all did for the
   Fatherland! Yes, I was a Nazi, yes I served my Führer and the
   Fatherland, and I'm proud, I had integrity. But this man, this
   blackmai ...

But the station tannoy drowns Drucker out.

TANNOY   The train approaching is the 7.15 from Durham.
   Please stand back, this Intercity train does not stop at this
   station ...

*Alan's eyes light up and he pushes Drucker onto the tracks, and
the train thunders over him, splashing blood all over Piers's
mackintosh and face.*

13. INT. DRUCKER'S LIVING ROOM. DAY.

*A little later. Alan has commandeered Drucker's house as the site
for a press conference. Piers stands at Alan's shoulder, in a neck
brace – obviously Alan has extracted retribution.*

ALAN   ... I thought he was a harmless old man. But when I
   realised he was a Nazi ...
   Alan pauses, and the press start clamouring.

WALLY CRASS   Wally Crass, *Daily Express*: so what's so wrong
   about being a Nazi? *(Gets no answer)*

PHIL GROSS   Phil Gross, *The Sun*: is there a sexual angle to all
   this, Al?

ALAN   No.

PHIL GROSS   Not to worry, we'll make one up.

JEFF DICQUEAD   Dicquead of *The Star*. Aren't you guilty of
   murder, technically speaking?

ALAN   Mr Dicquead, you must be *The Star*'s crack crime

reporter, judging by your incredible power of deductive logic! Yes, I pushed a Nazi killer under a train, so probably I am guilty of murder! And as the massed media were there to witness my crime of passion, no doubt tomorrow it will be splashed all over the world's papers.

PIERS *(Peevish)* It splashed all over my new raincoat!

ALAN Well, if my headstrong act catapults me into international fame, so be it. Shall we do the photos in here or outside?

14. INT. MUSSOLINI'S. DAY.

Next morning, and several power breakfasts are taking place. Piers Lonsdale sits at his usual table. The manager stands nearby, ready to do Piers Lonsdale's bidding. At present he is on the phone to a totty.

PIERS LONSDALE   I'm sorry, Caroline, but I haven't time for dinner and sexual intercourse, you'll have to choose. Okay, dinner it is, then. Eight thirty, Mussolini's. And to save time tonight I'll fax you the menu now. Ciao.

Piers Lonsdale takes a portable fax from his briefcase, taps out Caro's phone number, and feeds the menu in. Then Alan enters.

PIERS LONSDALE   Alan, morning. Coffee? Cocaine?

ALAN   No, let's have some champagne!

MANAGER   Certainly, sir. Of course, sir.

ALAN   Vintage. Magnum. Cold. Now. *(Manager scuttles off)* I must thank you for yesterday's advice, Piers.

PIERS LONSDALE   I don't recall giving you any stock market tips yesterday . . . ?

ALAN   No, your political advice. As a result, I've got twelve kilos of gold in the boot of my car, I'm about to become the world's most popular man, and I'll probably be driving A. Ford by teatime . . . that's 'A' for Anna . . .

PIERS LONSDALE   Really! You don't mean you actually found a Nazi!?

ALAN   You wait until you see the morning papers . . .

At this moment, Piers Fletcher Dervish arrives with all the morning papers under his arm.

ALAN   I'll let the headlines speak for me. *(Snatches papers from Piers, who drops most of them. Alan gives the couple he has seized to Piers Lonsdale)*

PIERS   *(Gathering up the other papers)* Alan, I've looked at the papers, and . . .

ALAN   Shut up, Piers. *(To Piers Lonsdale, who is glancing at the front pages with a puzzled look)* Well?

PIERS LONSDALE   'Prince Harry Has Nosebleed', *Daily Express* – 'President Reagan Was Alien From Outer Space', *The Guardian*. 'Mrs Thatcher Still Incredibly Super', *Daily Mail* . . . Nothing about you, old boy.

ALAN *(Snatches the papers from Piers Lonsdale)* What?! *(Looks at several front pages, then throws the papers down in disgust)* Yesterday, I pushed a Nazi war criminal under a train, in front of fifteen press photographers and a German TV crew! And not a word! *(Thinks)* The sods must have stuck me on the inside pages! *(Starts looking)*

PIERS There's nothing on the inside pages either, Alan, I've looked.

ALAN They can't do this! I'm a murderer! I demand press coverage! This is censorship!

PIERS LONSDALE Of course it is, I'm surprised you're so naive. Surely you know that the media are under strict

instructions from Number Ten not to print anything deroga-
tory about any Conservative politician, except Edward Heath.

ALAN   Bugger!

PIERS LONSDALE   Yes, that's the rumour they're trying to
spread.

Piers of the Realm

1. INT. ALAN'S SURGERY. DAY.

Alan is in his constituency for a rare visit, and is holding a surgery. This takes place in a shabby little office in the Conservative Association HQ, formerly a Victorian mansion. Alan, dressed to go racing, is finishing with a constituent, a ruddy faced farmer.

ALAN . . . I'll buy the Minister of Transport a drink, I'm sure I can persuade him to re-route the bypass around your farm . . .

FARMER *(Surprised and impressed)* Thank you very much, Mr B'Stard . . . *(Stands and starts to leave)*

ALAN Where do you think you're going, Walter Gabriel!?

FARMER Back home to tell Mrs Higginbotham the good news . . .

ALAN I think we've forgotten something.

FARMER I said thank you . . .

ALAN My fee!

FARMER But you're my MP!

ALAN So what? You'd pay any other specialist, wouldn't you? If I was a solicitor or a doctor or Cynthia Payne . . .

FARMER   But our old MP never used to charge!

ALAN   Yes, but that was B.T. − Before Thatcher. Come on,
cough up, five hundred pounds, or I'll make sure they turn
your entire farm into a motorway service area catering
exclusively for motor cycle gangs.

FARMER   But I haven't got five hundred pounds! We had a
very bad harvest!

ALAN   Yes, of course you did, and I suppose you stumbled
across that brand new Range Rover outside when you were
pulling up mongoloid wurzels, or whatever disgusting things
you farmers do. *(Angry farmer gets out chequebook)* Cash,
please, or else I have to charge you VAT.

FARMER   *(Gets large grubby bank roll out of pocket, and peels off ten
fifties)* That's the last time I vote Conservative!

ALAN   I'm quaking, that's my majority slashed to 26,736!

The farmer storms out, slamming the door. Alan starts counting the grubby notes. Then an old lady looks nervously round the door.

ALAN   Come back and clean later, I'm counting money.

MRS BICK   Oh, all right . . . *(Shuts door. A few seconds pass. Then she re-enters timidly)* No, I want to see you, sir, if you can spare me a moment.

ALAN   God! I only came up to Yorkshire to see my horse running in the St Leger, popped in because I left my field-glasses here last year, and suddenly I'm inundated with pathetic constituents too weak-willed and generally inferior to cope with their own problems! This is supposed to be a Conservative constituency! You're meant to stand on your own two feet! Sometimes I despair of this whole country, I really do! *(The old woman starts to cry)* For crying out loud! – oh, you are, aren't you? Look, sit down, and don't drip on the desk, it's just been French-polished! *(Pushes blotter over to catch her tears)*

MRS BICK   I'm sorry, sir, but I'm so desperate! If you don't help me, I'll put my head in the gas oven!

ALAN   Well, as a freedom lover, I don't think people should be prevented from choosing suicide if they think that's the right course . . . *(Raises voice)* Next!

MRS BICK   It's my house you see, sir.

ALAN   Are you still here? What do you want now, fifty pence for the gas meter?

MRS BICK   *(Oblivious)* It's just too big for me to look after, now my Harold's gone and the children have all emigrated . . . *(Alan yawns)* I don't think I could stand another winter, sir, the way the wind blows off the moors, and I just can't afford to heat the place, what with coal at five and fourpence a sack.

ALAN   What?

MRS BICK   *(Heedless)* And I hardly ever get out any more, not now petrol's up to three and ninepence a gallon. Mr Macmillan never considers us old folk when he puts the taxes up, he'll be old himself too, one day . . .

ALAN   *(Humouring her)* Yes, he is rather a young man in a hurry, isn't he? If only Mr Churchill hadn't called it a day . . .

MRS BICK   Exactly what I say, sir. So there am I, rattling about this draughty seven bedroom house . . .

ALAN   Seven bedrooms?

MRS BICK   Plus attics. And how can I be expected to maintain three acres of garden and a tennis court at my age?

ALAN   How indeed? *(Brain clicking)* Have you lived in your house very long?

MRS BICK   My husband bought it in 1948, for five thousand pounds, we were quite comfortably off then . . . not like now with all these terrible things going on, Suez, and Hungary, and Teddy Boys and that revolting Dickie Valentine! All I want to do is go and live with my sister in Australia . . . but I'm stuck with this big old house, sir . . .

ALAN   Yes, it must be an awful worry . . . no-one seems to want large detached houses with lots of land, nowadays. They all prefer those neat little prefabs with gnomes in the garden and a new Hillman Husky parked outside. Have you tried to sell the house?

MRS BICK   Oh yes, but as soon as I get on to the subject of Dickie Valentine − he's my pet hate − they show me the door.

ALAN   And with a seven bedroom house the last thing you need is another door. *(As if musing)* So your husband paid five thousand pounds? But of course, that was . . . 1948, over . . . eight years ago.

MRS BICK   It seems longer.

ALAN   So it must have depreciated somewhat. But look, why don't I phone an expert, and ask her advice? *(Dials on the old Bakelite phone)*

MRS BICK   Oh, thank you, sir! You're a gentleman, you put me in mind of Anthony Eden . . . *(Continues through first part of Alan's call)* it's a crying shame my daughters are all married off and living in South America, or else I'd introduce you like a shot sir, real goers they are, both of them . . .

ALAN   Hello, Julia? Alan? Look, I know it's difficult over the telephone . . . You've got such a dirty mind, Jules . . . I need a rough price guide for a seven bedroom Victorian house in Haltemprice, with three acres of garden . . . Okay . . .

MRS BICK   I phoned my eldest up the other week, I said what's the weather like in Peru? And she said 'if I've told you once I've told you a hundred times, it's Chile!' So I said, 'I'll knit you a pully . . .'

ALAN   Hello, Jules, still here . . . *(To Mrs Bick)* Will you be quiet you garrulous old bag?! *(Mrs Bick shuts up)* . . . Yes, it probably needs money spent . . . About two hundred and fifty? Thanks. *(Hangs up)* Dear oh dear, bad news, I'm afraid, two hundred and fifty. Savage depreciation.

MRS BICK   But the ship to Australia costs four hundred and fifty-three pounds seventeen and six!

ALAN   Yes, I suppose it must. Mmm, well, call me a soft hearted fool . . .

MRS BICK   You're a soft hearted f. . .

ALAN   SHUT UP!!

MRS BICK   Sorry sir . . .

ALAN   But I can't let a senile old bat like you suffer another terrible Yorkshire winter for the sake of two hundred pounds. Look, I know I'm being silly, but I'll buy the house . . .

MRS BICK   But you haven't even seen it sir!

ALAN   I know, but in my experience, cretins are generally honest; and I was elected to help people . . . *(Gets out the pile of notes he got from the farmer)* Here's five hundred pounds . . .

MRS BICK   *(Eyes light up)* Five hundred! Your War Bonds must have come up.

ALAN   Yes, but don't tell a soul, or else everyone will expect me to take their useless old houses off their hands. *(Crosses to door and opens it)* Leave the address with my secretary, I'll be round this afternoon with my solicitor . . .

MRS BICK   Thank you sir, God bless you sir . . .

Mrs Bick tries to kiss Alan's hand, which he snatches away. He ushers the old looney out, and crosses back to phone, which he lifts up, and dials.

ALAN   *Sunday Times?* Classified adverts, please . . . Hello . . .
Yes. 'For Sale. Victorian house of immense character. Seven
principal bedrooms, huge garden with tennis court, some
modernisation required, offers above two hundred and fifty
. . .' Of course that's thousand. What year do you think it is?
1956!? It's 'Exquisite Properties, Box 169, Haltemprice.'
That's right . . .

Alan hangs up, just as door swings open, and Sarah enters,
angry but gorgeously attired.

ALAN   Sarah, long time no see. I'd love to stay and chat, but
Eat the Poor is favourite for the St Leger . . .

SARAH   Alan, you summoned me to meet you here!

ALAN   Oh, that's right, of course . . . I wonder why I would
have done that?

SARAH   Perhaps to explain why you haven't paid my Harrods,
my Harvey Nickers, my Peter Jones, my Liberty, or my Yves
St Laurent accounts this month! And where have you been,
we haven't had any contact for weeks!

ALAN   I know. When I'm old I'll look back on these days as the
happiest of my entire marriage.

SARAH   Fine. That goes for me too, in spades! But that doesn't
give you the right to neglect me sartorially!

ALAN   On the other hand, my information suggests you spend
few of your waking hours fully dressed, and how much can
crotchless knickers cost?

SARAH   What are you talking about!?

ALAN   She said innocently. You don't know? Then here's a
clue. Since it was you who brought up the subject of spades,
how are you getting on with that muscular Jamaican gardener? What's his name, Capability Black? He certainly seems
capable.

SARAH   *(Starting to worry)* He's very er . . . hardworking.

ALAN   I know. *(Opens his overnight bag, removes a video cassette,*
and shows it to Sarah, but doesn't give it to her) People will
gossip in a small town like this, so I installed some discreet
video cameras. If only you'd been as discreet! Still, it's an ill

wind, you and Black Beauty are riding high, so to speak, in the German porno video charts – seems black and white movies are back in fashion. *(Exits, leaving a shocked Sarah)*

2. INT. COMMONS LOBBY. DAY.

A suntanned Alan walks jauntily through the Commons lobby. A journalist, yes it's Jeff Dicquead, sidles up to him.

DICQUEAD   Mr B'Stard! Alan! Jeff Dicquead . . .

ALAN   Oh yes, I remember you; *The Star*'s dimmest journalist.

DICQUEAD   You will have your little joke, won't you, Alan? Anyway, I've been promoted to political correspondent. So how was the holiday in Monte Carlo? Get your leg over much?

ALAN   I think that's for Princess Stephanie to answer.

DICQUEAD   Nice one! How many 'F's in Steffanie?

ALAN   About three.

DICQUEAD   Right . . . Crying shame your horse did so badly in the St Leger.

ALAN   Why, did you back him?

DICQUEAD   I had a thousand on the nose! Eat the Poor was the hot favourite, wasn't he?!

ALAN   Ah yes. But unfortunately, he was drugged just before the race . . .

DICQUEAD   Really? That's terrible!

ALAN   Especially for the people who didn't know in advance.

Alan grins and makes for the door to the chamber. Then Dicquead realises that Alan did him out of his winnings, and his face grows dark with anger.

3. INT. COMMONS CHAMBER. DAY.

Alan comes through from previous scene into an almost empty chamber, and takes his usual place on the backest bench just as the session is about to start. He sees Piers standing at the despatch box, nervously shuffling papers.

ALAN   *(Calls)* Piers, what are you doing down there?! You're a backbencher, you dunce! Come here before Black Rod gets his hands on you!

PIERS   *(Calls back)* No, it's all right Alan . . .

At this point, the Speaker calls them to order.

MR SPEAKER   Order! Order! *(The House quietens down)* Mr Piers Fletcher Dervish.

ALAN   *(Astounded)* What?!

Piers takes his place at the despatch box.

PIERS   Mr Speaker, I have here a statement from the Secretary of State for Housing. *(Reading carefully from notes)* As Honourable Members may have heard when the Prime Minister appeared on *The Jimmy Greaves Show* yesterday, we intend to introduce radical new legislation to deal once and for all with the housing crisis in our inner cities ...

ALAN   *(To no-one in particular)* I go away for a long weekend and this happens!

4. INT. LOBBY. DAY.

A while later, after the session. Piers comes briskly out of the chamber, talking to a civil servant. Alan chases after him and grabs his arm.

ALAN   Piers, what the hell's going on?!

PIERS   I'd have thought that was obvious, Alan. I've been promoted. While you were sunning yourself in the South of France, the Secretary of State for Housing personally asked for me as his junior minister!

ALAN   You?! Why?!

PIERS   Because I'm hardworking, honest and diligent, he said ...

ALAN   Yes, of course, but they put bigger brains into digital watches!

PIERS   *(With dignity)* Then why am I now a member of the Government, while you're still one of the ordinaries? *(Pokes out tongue)* Nahh! *(Alan opens his mouth to answer, but Piers doesn't let him)* Now I must be getting over to the Ministry, it doesn't do to be seen chatting to deadbeats. *(Passing members laugh. Alan seethes)* Besides, I'm so busy, I haven't even had time to clear my desk yet. *(Walks off with his civil servant)* Now, explain again the difference between a tenant and a rent boy ...

ALAN   *(Evilly)* I'll clear your desk for you, Piers ...

5. INT. ALAN'S OFFICE. DAY.

Alan enters the office in a wild-eyed state. On Piers's desk there are cardboard boxes half full of his possessions. Alan opens Piers's drawers, pulls them right out, and dumps the contents in the carboard boxes. Then, with increasing mania, he opens all of Piers's filing cabinet drawers and throws their contents onto Piers's desk. Then he starts chucking everything out of the window. He rips Piers's telephone off the wall and throws it through the window too. He notices Clarissa's framed photo on the desk, so he tears it from the frame and burns it in the ashtray. He rips all Piers's books apart, then finds, beneath all the debris, Piers's old teddy bear.

ALAN   You're Piers's bear, aren't you? You must know what's going on, he tells you everything!

Alan's eyes light up cruelly. He sits down, and sits the teddy on the table and ties its arms behind its back, with rubber bands. He turns on the anglepoise and shines it in the bear's eyes. Then he takes out a cigar, and lights it, and puffs until the end grows red.

ALAN   I think it's time we had a little chat, Mr Bear . . . Or shall I call you Teddy? Why has Piers Fletcher Dervish been made a Minister? Why him? Why not me? Why not you? You're cleverer than him! . . . So you won't talk, eh? *(Stabs the bear with the cigar)* Tell me! *(Stabs the bear again)* Why? Why?! *(But the bear says nothing)* All right, bear, you leave me no choice! *(Gets the scissors from his desk, and cuts off one of the bear's ears)* Tell me . . . ! What do you mean, you can't hear?! *(Shouts)* Tell me! Speak! *(Starts to cut off one of the bear's legs)* What's that?! Ah, of course, the Secretary of State promoted Piers *because* he's stupid! But why? You don't know, do you? Or maybe you do, maybe you and the Secretary of State are in cahoots, and Piers is your pawn! *(Takes bear and ties it to the hat stand, then gets tin of lighter fluid and douses the toy)* My patience is wearing thin bear, like your fur. Unless you give me some straight answers, you're Ted of Arc . . . No? On

your own fur be it. *(Sets fire to bear, and laughs manically as it goes up in flames)*

6. EXT. DEPARTMENT OF HOUSING. DAY.

Alan, briefcase in hand, walks up the street towards the D.O.H. building. Several cars are parked at parking meters. A traffic warden is coming towards Alan. Alan takes a coin from his pocket and feeds one of the meters, just as the warden comes abreast.

WARDEN   You shouldn't have done that, sir. Don't you know it's illegal to feed the meter? *(Starts writing ticket)*

ALAN   I know that, but it's not my car.

Alan laughs as the car receives a ticket under the windscreen wiper. He goes on to the ornate entrance of the Ministry. Propped against the wall is a one-legged beggar, aged about twenty-five, whose ragged coat bears some medals. On the ground is his old army beret and a sign which reads: 'As seen on Tumbledown *— BBC1'.*

BEGGAR   Have you got fifty pence for a cup of tea, sir?

ALAN   Yes thank you. *(Enters the building grinning)*

7. INT. HOUSING MINISTER'S OFFICE. DAY.

A large, comfortable office, containing heavy furniture and quite good pictures from the civil service art collection. There's room for a desk and chairs, as well as a couple of armchairs either side of a fireplace. Piers is sitting behind the big desk, watching Tickle on the Tum *on the ministerial television, with great enjoyment. The latest edition of* The Beano *is on the desk. Then the intercom buzzes. Piers makes several attempts to find the right button, finally doing so.*

PIERS   Yes?

FEMALE VOICE   Mr B'Stard's here to see you, Minister.

PIERS   Say that again.

FEMALE VOICE   *(Louder)* Mr B'Stard's here to see you, Minister.

PIERS   I love it when you call me that, Judith! Does he have an appointment?

ALAN'S VOICE   I don't need an appointment to see you, you nincompoop!

PIERS   Oh don't you? All right, you'd better come in.

Piers turns the television off, puts his Beano *in the desk drawer, and opens the first file in his in-tray, as Alan enters, at his smarmiest.*

ALAN   Piers, super office, gorgeous secretary. Sauced her yet?
PIERS   Alan! I've only been here two days.
ALAN   Well you know what they say, Piers: a secretary is just another piece of office equipment, you can't be sure she's yours until she's been screwed on the desk.
FEMALE VOICE   *(Through intercom)* How dare you!?
PIERS   Oooops. *(Turns the intercom off)* Actually, it's not my office, it's the Secretary of State's. But Sir Greville is away opening a new housing estate . . . in the Seychelles.

ALAN   Did he take the key to the drinks cabinet with him?

PIERS   Of course not.

ALAN   Open it, then, open it!

Piers unlocks the drinks cabinet. Alan removes a brandy bottle and a large balloon, and pours himself a proper drink.

ALAN   Would you like one?

PIERS   I shouldn't, drink fuddles the brain.

ALAN   Piers, I never knew you were an alcoholic! *(Raises his glass)* Cheers, here's to you . . . Minister.

PIERS   Thank you, Alan. I'm sorry I was rude to you in the lobby . . .

ALAN   Yes, it was completely out of order, Piers. You don't know how much you upset me. Frankly, I had to fight back the tears. I consider you my friend, Piers, and to think you abandoned me . . .

PIERS   I'm sorry Alan . . .

ALAN   I should have expected it. They say power corrupts. And you are now a very powerful man.

PIERS   Yes, I suppose I am.

ALAN   So what actually are your duties?

PIERS   I can't tell you that, Alan. Official Secrets.

ALAN   Piers, I'm your friend. And I don't want details, just the general outlines . . .

PIERS   Oh, all right. I'm in charge of listed buildings. All applications by owners of old or architecturally important buildings come to me, and it's awfully important, because there are grants and things you can apply for. Suppose you owned an old castle, and it was falling down . . .

ALAN   Yes, I see . . .

PIERS   . . . and you wanted money to stop it falling down, or you wanted to replace a thatched roof . . .

ALAN   Yes, right . . .

PIERS   Not that castles have thatched roofs, I've already learned that much, but if you owned a medieval long house, or a prehistoric stone circle . . .

At this moment the division bell sounds.

ALAN   Saved by the bell!

PIERS   Come on, Alan, we'd better get a move on!

ALAN   What is it? Fire drill?

PIERS   No, the division bell, we have to vote!

ALAN   I don't think I can be bothered, it's only some tedious private member's bill about lung disease in miners . . . go on, I'll look after the departmental brandy.

Piers nods, and rushes out. Alan grins, and crosses to the door and locks it. Then he hurries over to the desk, and starts looking through the in-tray. He discards the first few items, then comes to an interesting letter. He reads it out.

ALAN   'Dear Minister, can you help me, sir, 1 am desperate. Last month, I visited my MP to ask his help in disposing of my old house. He pretended to help, but in fact he did me out of a quarter of a million pounds . . .'

Alan laughs, and puts the letter through the desk top shredder. Then he sees the file Piers left open. He starts reading it.

ALAN   '. . . applications for renovation grants for newly listed historic monuments . . . Belvedere Hostel, Paddington . . . the De La Rue Hotel, Notting Hill . . . the Elite Sauna Parlour, Greek Street . . . *(With mounting disbelief)* Beaver Videos, Wardour Street . . . !'

There is a rattling at the door.

PIERS *(O.O.V)*   Alan!

ALAN   *(Closes file and unlocks the door)* That was quick!

PIERS   It *was* a fire drill . . . *(Goes back to his chair and sits)*

ALAN   *(Perches on the desk)* Piers, what were we talking about before? Oh, I remember, historic buildings.

PIERS   That's right, did I tell you I have to approve all the . . . ?

ALAN   Yes, you went into considerable detail. But I must admit that when I think of historic buildings, I think of great national monuments. The Tower of London, St Paul's Cathedral, Hatfield House, Windsor Davies, rather than the Belvedere Hotel, Paddington, the De La Rue Hotel, Notting

Hill, the Elite Sauna Parlour, Greek Street, Beaver Videos . . .

PIERS   B for videos! Some people can't even spell! Hold on, you've been looking at my files!

ALAN   Only as a friend. I think someone's taking liberties with you, Piers. Why should you give historic monument grant status to a string of brothels, strip clubs and doss houses? Someone is using you to rubber stamp all these illegitimate applications. The question is, who?

PIERS   I can't tell you that, Alan.

ALAN   Of course, Official Secrets.

PIERS   No, that's not the reason. You think I was born yesterday, don't you?

ALAN   My money's on the small hours of this morning.

PIERS   Well I wasn't. I know the ropes, you don't want to be taken in by this dumb act. You think I'm really stupid, getting me to do terrible things for you, awful evil favours, but I've bided my time, I've kept my wits about me . . . and now I've got power, and I know what power is worth. If you want to know who these buildings belong to, it'll cost you!

ALAN   You're asking for . . . ?!

PIERS   That's right, Alan, even Piers Fletcher Dervish is corruptible. I know how the machine is oiled. There's dirty money about, and I want my share!

ALAN   *(Amazed)* A bribe?

PIERS   Why not? I've got the information you want, and that costs money.

ALAN   How much?

PIERS   One pound fifty.

ALAN   One pound fifty?

PIERS   Cash.

ALAN   *(Fighting laughter)* You're a hard man, Piers . . . solid bone from the neck up. *(Hands over two coins)*

PIERS   And don't you forget it. All right, all these properties belong to my boss, Sir Greville McDonald, the Secretary of State for Housing.

ALAN   Thank you, Piers, that's all I wanted to know. *(About to leave)* By the way, you left your teddy bear in the office.

PIERS   Oh, thank God, I've been looking everywhere for my Pooh! He's irreplaceable, I've had him since I was born, and he was Daddy's before . . .

Piers tails off as Alan takes a plastic bag from his briefcase and empties the scorched remnants of Pooh onto Piers's desk.

ALAN   Next time we meet in the lobby, Piers, just remember who's really your boss.

Piers is stunned. Alan leaves grinning. Then Piers starts to cry. The intercom goes.

FEMALE VOICE   Minister, the Under Secretary would like a few moments . . .

PIERS   *(Sobbing hysterically)* He's burnt my teddy . . . ee . . . ee . . . ee . . . ee . . . !

8. INT. ALAN'S OFFICE. DAY.

The office is empty, and in a terrible mess from Alan's trashing of Piers's possessions. There is a figure hanging from the light fixture. Closer inspection shows the figure consists of some old clothes of Piers's, topped with a face cut out of one of Piers's election photographs. The phone rings twice, then an answerphone cuts in, in Alan's voice.

ALAN'S VOICE   Hello, it's your immense good fortune to be listening to the recorded voice of Alan B'Stard MP, largest majority in the House of Commons. I'm far too important to wait about for you to call, but leave a message, and if it's interesting enough, I may deign to ring back, reversing the charges, naturally. Speak after the high pitched tone obtained by my tweaking Piers Fletcher-Dervish's private member's bill. *(Eeeek!)*

GERMAN VOICE   Alan, you wacky Englisher! This is Hörst. Listen, *Sarah's Sex Garden* is the toast of Hamburg, number one in the porno charts! We must make a follow-up, big budget, colour, music by James Last. We could clean up the Christmas market, well, dirty up ... and they say the Germans have no sense of humour!

9. INT. ALAN'S DRAWING ROOM. DAY.

A couple of days later. Alan and Sarah are finishing lunch. Alan is being terribly effusive and nice — Sarah is wary, but starting to relax.

ALAN   ... And I read in *Vogue* that the new collection of Christian Dior silk lingerie is on sale now at their Bond Street boutique. Apparently smoky grey is THE colour for winter, you should treat yourself ... More champagne?

SARAH   *(Holds out her glass)* Thank you.

ALAN   And isn't your full length Russian sable coat looking a little shabby? Perhaps you should have a new one.

SARAH   Alan, I never thought I'd say this, but stop trying to buy me things!

ALAN   I just want to make it up to you, darling.

SARAH   And I've accepted all your apologies ...

ALAN   They're not enough. My behaviour towards you was dishonourable, vindictive, brutal ... I was driven mad with jealousy, you see, the thought of you with another man, let alone a semi-skilled gardener on a job creation scheme!

SARAH   But I didn't ... !

ALAN   I know you didn't, my love, I should never have listened to vicious gossip. I've written a stiff letter to the Women's Institute, I can tell you.

SARAH   Then you don't want me to sack the gardener?

ALAN   On the contrary, you must give Capability a big rise ...

SARAH   His name's Vince ...

ALAN   And perhaps you should take on some more gardeners, and a chauffeur, maybe a gamekeeper ... We should do more for the disadvantaged, we can afford to employ a houseful of strong young men to take care of your needs when I'm away ... *(Drains his glass and stands)* I wish I could come shopping with you and your new Platinum Card, but I have an important meeting this afternoon ... *(Kisses her on forehead, makes for door)*

SARAH *(Wary)* So what was in that video tape that you waved at me in Haltemprice?

ALAN I don't know, I just picked it up in Woolworth's ... Rag Tag and Bobtail, I think. You knew it couldn't be you and Vince!?

Sarah laughs charmingly. Alan exits. Sarah crosses to phone and dials a number.

SARAH Hello, Vince? Sweetie, you can have your job back, Alan doesn't know after all! *(There's a buzz on the entryphone. Assuming Alan's forgotten something, she presses the button)* And are your brothers still on the dole? Lovely!

Then the door opens, and Jeff Dicquead enters. Sarah puts the phone down in surprise.

SARAH Who are you?!

DICQUEAD Jeff Dicquead, *The Star*.

SARAH My husband's just left.

DICQUEAD Yeah, just left of Genghis Khan. *(Laughs at his own joke)* Actually, I've been waiting for him to leave. It's you I want to talk to, on a matter of delicacy ...

SARAH And what exactly is this ... ?

DICQUEAD Matter of delicacy? Well, how to put this tactfully? *(Thinks)* Yeah. Do you deny you are the star of the hottest porno flick on sale in Hamburg today?

SARAH What ... ?! Yes!

DICQUEAD What, you admit ... ?!

SARAH No, I deny it, you asked me if I deny it, and I do! Now get out!

DICQUEAD Hold on, what do you say about this?! *(He produces from his raincoat pocket a video box with* Sarah's Sex Garden *emblazoned on the cover) Sarah's Sex Garden.* I have to hand it to you, it's bloody brilliant!

SARAH Get out!

DICQUEAD   I only watched ten minutes, and I was as hard as Rupert Murdoch was on the printers!

SARAH   It's not me! It's a terrible video libel!

DICQUEAD   No, I'm sorry love, I'm sure it is you, you've got a very distinctive mole on your left buttock. Mind you, that's the risk you run, doing it on the lawn.

SARAH   *(Trying to push him out of the room)* Get out, get out!

DICQUEAD   Oh, don't be such a spoil-sport, love. Come on, we're all adults, I'm not moralising, I like a good stag film as much as the next man . . . In fact, I've always wanted to do it with a porno queen, come on, give us a little squeeze . . . *(Sarah smiles coldly, comes close to him, reaches her hand into his groin, and squeezes and squeezes and squeezes until he falls to his knees in agony)* Oh, magic! *(And he passes out)*

10. INT. HOUSING MINISTER'S OFFICE. DAY.

Alan is confronting the Secretary of State for Housing, Sir Greville McDonald, an urbane gent. The mood is very civilised, with cups of tea and butter osborne biscuits, but both crooks know where they stand.

ALAN   . . . So you asked for Piers as your junior minister, knowing he is the missing link between the animal and vegetable kingdoms?

MINISTER   The PM agreed with my recommendation; she likes unambitious men in her Government.

ALAN   Then you're unambitious?

MINISTER\   In political terms . . .

ALAN   But not when it comes to feathering your nest? Unless my information is incorrect and William Shakespeare really was a patron of the Elite Sauna Parlour?

MINISTER   I suppose it's money you want?

ALAN   Certainly not. I just want you to authorise a few of my slum properties for expensive refurbishment. For example, I've just bought a large tenement building in Kennington, and I'm almost sure Henry VIII used to crash there when he'd had a skinful, and he knew Catherine of Aragon was waiting at Hampton Court with the royal rolling pin.

MINISTER   Why don't I get Fletcher Dervish to give you some signed blanks and you can just fill them in and forward them to the Paymaster General?

ALAN   Thank you, Minister. It's a pleasure doing business with an honest criminal.

MINISTER   Likewise. *(They shake hands, and he leads Alan to the door)* Perhaps we'll sit alongside each other in Cabinet one day . . . *(Shows Alan out. Shuts door)* . . . if you're spared.

11. EXT. DEPARTMENT OF HOUSING. DAY.

Alan comes down the front steps. The beggar accosts him.

BEGGAR   Please Captain, I haven't eaten for two weeks . . .

ALAN   Well force yourself.

A happy Alan walks across the road. Suddenly shots ring out. The first bullets shatter the windscreen of a parked car. Then half a dozen bullets smash into Alan's chest. Blood spurts, as Alan bounces off the car bonnet, hits the pavement and lies still.

We see a tiny figure watching from an upstairs window of the Department of Housing. We zoom in (to a studio shot) to see the Minister, smiling and holding a rifle.

Then we spot Sarah at a table at a pavement cafe. She is putting a small pearl handled revolver back into her Louis Vuitton handbag.

But then we notice Piers skulking behind a parked car, with an army officer's Browning in his hand. He drops it down a drain.

We see an elderly lady in a distant telephone box. We zoom in (to studio shot) to reveal Mrs Bick, removing the telephoto sight from an Uzzi sub-machine gun.

Finally we see the beggar blowing the smoke away from the end of his steel crutch, which is actually a Day of the Jackal *type rifle.*

Some passers-by hurry over to Alan, but he's quite dead. We hear a distant ambulance.

Roll final credits, without music. Under them, we hear a newscaster's voice.

NEWSCASTER   . . . it happened at 3.47pm, as Mr B'Stard was coming out of the Department of Housing. He was rushed to Charing Cross Hospital, but was found to be . . .

Silence

The reason why Alan B'Stard faked his own murder is far too intriguing for us to be allowed to give away in this slim volume. You may, however, find out in the next volume – or the one after that – you'll just have to keep on buying . . .

Labour of Love

1. INT. ALAN'S OFFICE. DAY.

Afternoon, day one. Alan and Piers are going through opened constituency mail, Alan is feeding his letters straight into a shredder.

ALAN *(Glances at letter)* 'Wife needs open heart surgery.' *(Shreds letter)* 'I'm unemployed and can't afford to feed my family.' *(Shreds it)* God, why do these constituents keep bothering me?!

PIERS But Alan, it's our duty to help. I'm raising money in my constituency to buy a kidney machine for our local hospital. So far I've received a thousand pounds. *(Shows Alan a stack of bank notes on his desk)*

ALAN You mean they just send you money? Brilliant scam!

PIERS It's not a scam, Alan! If we don't show we care we won't get re-elected.

ALAN We're not going to get re-elected, Piers. I mean the Prime Minister's a megalomaniac and the Cabinet's full of non-entities . . .

Sir Greville has entered during this last speech. Sir Greville wears horn rimmed bifocals. With him is a fat young man —

Victor Crosby MP. Sir Greville coughs, Alan whirls.

ALAN   *(Smarm)* Sir Greville . . .

PIERS   Hello Sir Greville, new glasses? They really suit you!

SIR GREVILLE   *(To Crosby)* Told you he was an inveterate crawler, didn't I? Actually they're my spare pair, I've mislaid my others . . .

PIERS   Were you wearing them when you came in here? Oh no, you wouldn't have been, would you? *(Alan kicks Piers)* Perhaps you dropped them, I'll look.

Piers starts crawling round on the floor. Alan pockets the thousand pounds on Piers's desk.

ALAN   *(Sizing up Crosby)* And who might you be?

SIR GREVILLE   This, gentlemen, is Victor Crosby the hero of last week's Accrington by-election.

ALAN   *(Instant dislike to newcomer)* I didn't know the EC butter mountain was eligible to stand for Parliament.

PIERS   *(Jumps up, excited. Bangs head on desk, then pumps Victor's hand)* You're Victor Crosby, you were in my newspaper!

ALAN   The last time I had something that white and flabby in my newspaper, it had just been fried in batter.

SIR GREVILLE   You mustn't mind B'Stard, his political career's nearly over and failure has made him bitter.

CROSBY   *(Mock surprise)* You're Alan B'Stard?! They told me you were good looking. *(Sits behind Alan's desk)* Is this the desk then, Greville? Rather small, isn't it? Still, you know what they say; 'like prick, like desk.' *(Sir Greville shoots him a glance that says 'don't be indiscreet'. Piers laughs)*

CROSBY   *(Swivels in chair)* Still, I suppose it'll do until I get my first ministerial post.

SIR GREVILLE   Victor, don't be so hasty. You must expect to spend at least three months on the backbenches first. *(Goes to leave)* Perhaps I left them in the tea room. *(Leaves)*

Piers sits at his desk, and sniggers at Alan's downfall. Alan darts over, opens the top drawer, pushes Piers's hand in and slams the drawer shut.

PIERS   Ow! Ow! Ow!

ALAN   *(Tips Piers out of his chair on to the floor)* All right, Piers, shift!

Alan takes over Piers's desk, sweeping all Piers's papers onto the floor. Piers sucks his hurt hand. The phone rings on Alan's desk.

ALAN
CROSBY   Get that Piers.

PIERS   Hello? Yes . . . Hold on . . . It's the *Sunday Express*, they

want to speak to the most right-wing Tory in Parliament . . .

ALAN *(Goes for phone)* Out of the way, Crosby . . .

CROSBY *(Beats Alan to phone)* Hello, Victor Crosby speaking
. . . That's right, the conqueror of Accrington . . . How much
do you usually pay B'Stard? Pathetic! Double it and add a
nought or two! You want a quote for publicity? Okay. People
held hostage by Muslim extremists should be left to rot
before we give in to political blackmail. *(Puts the phone down)*

ALAN Call that radical!? I say, round up all the Arabs in
England, and shoot one a day until our hostages are free! And
Salman Rushdie'll be first against the wall, because it's all his
fault!

CROSBY Pathetic! We should implant a bomb in the head of
everyone going abroad, designed to explode if they're kept in
a dark room for more than a day! *(Alan opens his mouth to top
Crosby, decides Crosby is too unstable to be topped, and thinks better
of it)* And then we should use our Army to take out those
double-dealing, sheep murdering Frenchies once and for all.

PIERS I once took out a Frenchie, but she wanted to kiss with
her mouth open, and I wasn't wearing a contraceptive.

CROSBY Did he escape from some sort of political asylum!?

ALAN There's nothing wrong with Piers! He's a valuable
member of our great Conservative movement!

PIERS Am I really, Alan?

ALAN Of course. With you on our side no one can say the
Conservatives discriminate against the mentally handicapped.

CROSBY Or the physically under endowed?

ALAN *(Taken aback)* How did you . . . ? *(Stops himself, but can't
help looking at his crotch. Then he storms out)*

2. INT. ALAN'S BATHROOM. DAY.

*Morning, day two. Sarah is in the shower cubicle. The shower is
en suite to the bedroom. The door from the bedroom opens and
Alan enters in his office clothes.*

ALAN   Hello . . .

SARAH   Who is it?

ALAN   Who is it?! What kind of question is that?! *(Marches to shower door and pulls it open)*

SARAH   *(Slips bathrobe on)* Oh it's you. Where did you spend last night?

ALAN   I had an all night sitting.

SARAH   I hope you didn't suffocate the poor girl . . .

ALAN   And then I stayed at my club.

SARAH   I didn't know they had rooms at the Soho Peeperama.

ALAN   *(Cold anger)* Sarah, I'm not in the mood for your cabaret act. Why did you tell Victor Crosby I've got a small penis?

SARAH   I'm sorry, Alan. I just bumped into him in Fortnum's tea room, conversation flagged . . .

ALAN   You're having an affair with him, aren't you?

SARAH   Alan, of course I'm not. He's fat, ugly and he's got greasy hair.

ALAN   So? Didn't stop you with Nigel Lawson.

SARAH   But he was rich.

ALAN   Fair point . . . You're really not having an affair with Crosby?

SARAH   Of course not . . . Mr Caterpillar. Why are you so obsessed with Victor Crosby?

ALAN   I hate him. He's got my desk, my newspaper column, he's Sir Greville's blue-eyed rat . . . He'll be in the Cabinet soon! Mind you, who hasn't?

SARAH   *(Nastily)* You haven't. And with your political record you've got more chance of getting into the Labour Cabinet. *(Alan acknowledges this, even thinks that might be an interesting scam)* Shall I get dressed or do you want me to do something about that angry swelling?

ALAN   *(Looks down, surprised for a second that the conversation has aroused him)* Oh, all right, I'll just get the ointment.

Sarah goes through to the bedroom. Alan opens the medicine cabinet and sees a familiar pair of half moon glasses. Alan takes the glasses, is about to angrily twist them into pieces, then thinks better of it and slips them into a pocket.

3. EXT. LABOUR PARTY HQ. NIGHT.

Night. Day two. Alan walks along Walworth Road, collar turned up. He is approached by two threatening muggers, white with broad Yorkshire accents, who pull a switch blade and push him up against a wall.

MUGGER 1   Wallet time, mother!

ALAN   I beg your pardon, I don't speak unemployed.

MUGGER 1   I ain't jiving man!

ALAN   Aren't you? Okay, okay . . . *(Gives him wallet. The muggers run off)* 'I ain't jiving man!' I blame *Miami Vice*.

The muggers run down the road. Alan takes a little electronic gadget from his pocket, points it at the muggers and presses a button. The wallet explodes, the muggers disintegrate, windows are blown out, car alarms go off etc. Alan chuckles, and walks a few yards to Labour Party HQ. He goes up to the front door. A sign says 'The Labour Party. Smart Casual Dress Please. No

Hawkers, No Canvassers, No Socialists.' Alan looks around, and gives a secret knock. The door opens.

4. INT. PADDY O'ROURKE'S OFFICE. NIGHT.

Paddy O'Rourke, tough looking man in his fifties, in smart casual dress, sits behind a big desk. A large pile of plastic red roses in a box on the desk. There are lots of Labour Party posters on the wall, some quite old. Also pictures and busts of past leaders, a big union banner etc. Alan prowls round the office during the first part of the scene, sneering at the things he sees.

ALAN   What a perfectly vile little office.

PADDY O'ROURKE   *(Surprisingly well spoken)* It suffices. Now, let's get down to cases. We're taking a considerable risk having you here, I hope it's worth it. Well?

ALAN   Hold on, hold on! Where's all your Paddy O'Rourke Irish blarney that so enthrals the Labour Party conference?

PADDY O'ROURKE   I just do that to patronise the party faithful. Between you, me and the bust of Glynis Kinnock, I'm not even Irish!

ALAN   I can't see a bust of Glynis Kinnock . . .

PADDY O'ROURKE   No, I was just thinking about it.

ALAN   What?!

PADDY O'ROURKE   You're not the only one who likes a good . . . *(Stops himself)* Look, B'Stard, our research shows Labour only gets into power when it's led by chaps with a regional accent. Gaitskell and Foot were posh — what happened at the polls? Massacred. *(Crosses to bust or picture of Wilson)* But Ramsey McDonald and Harold Wilson put on the old patois, and bingo!

ALAN   What do you mean 'put on'?

PADDY O'ROURKE   For instance, everyone thinks Wilson's a Yorkshireman.

ALAN   Isn't he?

PADDY O'ROURKE   Comes from Basingstoke. And Ramsey McDonald was French. So we all decided Neil should get some Nye Bevan records out of the library and become Welsh. Now, you said on the phone you had something important for us? What is it?

ALAN   It's me. I want to join the Labour Party.

PADDY O'ROURKE   You!? You're the most right-wing Tory in the House — *(Alan grins)* after Victor Crosby! *(Alan's grin vanishes)* Look, this is all very suspect, how do I know it isn't a Tory dirty trick?

ALAN   They wouldn't send me, would they? They'd send someone like Peter Walker. He's so wet they call him Flipper.

PADDY O'ROURKE   But why join Labour? You're ahead in the polls . . . ?

ALAN   I know, but being a Tory is so boring now that Maggie's gone! I mean, have you ever had a conversation with John Major?

PADDY O'ROURKE   No . . .

ALAN   Neither have I. I've tried, but I always doze off. I won't say he's dull, but he is the first man ever to run away from the circus to join a firm of accountants.

PADDY O'ROURKE   Yes, but Thatcher was humdrum and common until Thaatchi and Thaatchi made her over. Once Major's had the treatment — new voice, new hair, new clothes, new handbag . . .

ALAN   But I can tilt the balance! I can get you hot inside information, manifesto leaks, copies of secret strategic briefing papers . . . !

PADDY O'ROURKE   In exchange for what? We haven't any money, it all goes on dialect coaching. John Smith is taking ages overcoming that Eton accent . . .

ALAN   Paddy old bean, I don't need your money.

PADDY O'ROURKE   Then what do you want?

ALAN   I want to be in the Labour Cabinet.

PADDY O'ROURKE   What?! What about abandoning your heartfelt political principles?

ALAN   What heartfelt political principles?

PADDY O'ROURKE   Of course, silly me.

ALAN   Well? Are you going to take up this once in a life time offer?

PADDY O'ROURKE   I'm sure I could persuade Glynis to sway Neil into finding you some sort of post . . . *(Starts tapping on his lap top)*

ALAN   Ideally I want a job with plenty of influence, glamour and travel, but not too much actual work.

PADDY O'ROURKE   How about Minister of Sport? *(Alan makes a dismissive face)* Or a Bishopric, they'll be in Neil's gift.

ALAN   No, I want the Foreign Office.

PADDY O'ROURKE   But we've got Kauffman down for that.

ALAN   Tough.

PADDY O'ROURKE   What do you know about foreign affairs?

ALAN   I've had more affairs with foreigners than you've had changes of policy!

PADDY O'ROURKE   Fair enough. *(Taps on keyboard)* Alan B'Stard, Foreign Secretary . . . Gerald Kaufman, Bishop of Bath and Wells.

ALAN   Well, it's been a pleasure doing treachery with you, see you in Downing Street . . . *(Stands)*

PADDY O'ROURKE   Hold on − how about some tangible sign of goodwill? When do we start seeing all these leaked documents?

ALAN   I couldn't have shown these to you last month, but . . . *(Takes some letters from inside pocket)* Mrs Thatcher's secret love letters to Gazza! Don't read them under the sprinklers though, they're red hot!

PADDY O'ROURKE   *(Opens first letter)* Bloody hell . . . ! No wonder he was in tears!

5. INT. ALAN'S OFFICE. NIGHT.

Night. Day two. Alan returns from his trip to Walworth Road. The room is empty. He sits at his old desk, idly tries the top drawer. It's locked. Alan tries his keys, but Crosby has changed the locks. Alan picks the top drawer lock with a paper clip. Alan rifles through the top drawer, and finds the typescript of Crosby's article for the Sunday Express.

ALAN   *(Reads aloud)* 'Towards a New Economic Miracle – the Case for Slavery. By Victor Crosby.'

Alan puts his feet up on the desk and starts to read Crosby's article. He reads odd phrases out aloud.

ALAN   '. . . Slavery keeps down wages by creating a large unpaid work force . . . reduces population growth by splitting up families . . . eliminates travel congestion by making slaves sleep at the workplace, simultaneously solving the housing crisis . . .' *(Grins)* I'm glad I wrote this.

Alan crosses to photocopier and copies the article. He puts it back in Crosby's desk, takes a mousetrap from under the desk, puts it in the drawer under some papers, and as he is re-locking the drawer, Piers enters.

PIERS   Hello, Alan! You just missed a really smashing debate on the environment. *(Takes an apple from pocket)* Did you know that leaded petrol can cause brain damage?
ALAN   Then you must have been bottle-fed on four star.
PIERS   Crosby was brilliant. He makes you look like a wet.

Piers bites into his apple. Alan suddenly leaps on Piers and forces the entire apple into Piers's mouth, gagging him.

ALAN   Take that back, Piers!
PIERS   *(Choking)* Nnn nnn!!
ALAN   Say sorry . . .
PIERS   Nnn nnnn NNN!!!
ALAN   I don't think we're talking the same language, Piers.

In desperation, Piers scrawls 'I'm sorry' on a scratch pad.

ALAN   Apology accepted. *(Alan slaps Piers on the back. The apple shoots out of his mouth and breaks a window)* Fifty pounds for the window, Piers.
PIERS   *(Giving Alan a fifty pound note)* Sorry, Alan.
ALAN   So, did Sir Greville wet his pants too, over Crosby's exciting and brilliant contribution?
PIERS   I don't know, Alan, he wasn't there . . .

ALAN   But he's Secretary of State ... Maybe he was off looking for his glasses ... or perhaps he was opening something ...

6. INT. ALAN'S DRAWING ROOM. NIGHT.

The door opens, and Sir Greville enters the empty room. He has his red box with him. He puts it down, and helps himself to a drink. He seems very much at home. He calls out.

SIR GREVILLE   Hello ...
SARAH   *(O.O.V.)* Who is it?
SIR GREVILLE   It's me, Grevvy ...
SARAH   *(O.O.V.)* Hang on a second darling, I'm just changing a fuse ... *(Sudden sound of electrical hum)* Ready.
SIR GREVILLE   *(Crosses to door, clearly he can see her)* I say ... !

7. INT. ALAN'S CAR. NIGHT.

Alan's car is parked down his street. He turns on a little radio receiver. The house is bugged, of course.

SIR GREVILLE   ... and you're sure he's not coming home tonight?
SARAH   *(V/O)* Don't worry, it's Tuesday, Alan's S&M night.
SIR GREVILLE   *(V/O)* Good, because I'd hate our coitus to be suddenly interruptus ...
ALAN   I won't disturb you ...
SARAH   *(V/O)* Let's go to bed ...

Alan grins wolfishly, turns off the receiver and gets out of the car.

SIR GREVILLE   *(V/O)* I hope that thing's earthed?
SARAH   *(V/O)* Of course it isn't, the electric shock's half the fun.

8. INT. ALAN'S DRAWING ROOM. NIGHT.

Alan creeps in. The room is empty. Then ...

SIR GREVILLE *(Suddenly in doorway)* Won't be a sec, darling, there's a packet of three in my trouser pocket ...

Alan hides.

SARAH *(V/O)* There's a machine in the bathroom.

Sir Greville disappears. Alan breathes a sigh of relief. Sir Greville's red box and trousers are on the floor. Alan gets Sir Greville's keys from his trousers, unlocks the red box, takes out some papers, relocks the red box.

ALAN Great, S&M night, and I nearly forgot. *(Makes whiplash noise and exits)*

9. INT. ALAN'S OFFICE. DAY.

Mid morning, day three. Alan sits at Piers's desk, about to write in a huge quilted Valentine card. Crosby enters.

ALAN Bing! Congratulations, I hear your maiden speech last night was absolutely brilliant.

CROSBY What are you after?!

ALAN Don't be so prickly! I'm offering my heartfelt acclaim! People are saying it was the best maiden speech since, well, mine.

CROSBY You?! I've heard better speakers attached to a five pound transistor radio!

ALAN Ha ha, Victor ... Vic ... I'll never have that sort of quick fire political wit. People are already talking about you as a future Prime Minister.

CROSBY I know, whereas they talk about you as a future Deputy Chairman of the Toilets Committee.

ALAN *(Swallows again)* That wit again! Mrs Thatcher was only saying over breakfast that if you'd been elected a year earlier, she wouldn't have had to endorse that John Major, the Prince of Greyness.

CROSBY You had breakfast with . . . Her!?
ALAN Yes, we're very close now. She's come to see, too late, who really loves her.

CROSBY I love her! I cried all night when that vile malcontent Heseltine turned against her.
ALAN Don't worry, Victor, we aren't alone, you and I . . . *(Arm around his shoulders, very confidential)* What do you know about the November 22nd Movement?
CROSBY November 22nd? The day she was ousted?
ALAN Exactly. The Movement is a hard core of dedicated

Thatcherite loyalists sworn to . . . No, I can't tell you . . .

CROSBY She's coming back, isn't she? She'll rise again! How do I join? How do I join?!

ALAN First you have to win her trust.

CROSBY *(Wily)* You said she admires me?

ALAN *(Quickly)* She does! But she doesn't know how you feel about her . . .

CROSBY There must be some way I can let her know?

ALAN *(As if he's just thought of it)* You could send her a Valentine card with a coded message of support!

CROSBY A Valentine card? Brilliant idea B'Stard . . . Alan . . . *(Thinks and becomes suspicious)* Why are you doing this for me?

ALAN Because you're going to the top, and I want to be there with you. Imagine what we could do together. *(Puts his arm round Vic's shoulder again)* We could abolish the NHS . . .

CROSBY Yes!

ALAN Disenfranchise women . . .

CROSBY Magnificent!

ALAN Re-introduce slavery . . .

CROSBY That's exactly what I was going to say in my *Sunday Express* article! You're really on my wavelength!

ALAN *(Modest)* Perhaps, but you broadcast a much stronger signal. Yes, you could become a key protagonist in the November 22nd Movement, if only . . .

CROSBY If only what?

ALAN If only you weren't such a ragamuffin! She likes her boys nicely turned out. Parkinson, Baker, me, we all have our suits made in Savile Row. Where's yours from? MFI?

CROSBY *(Looks at label on inside pocket)* Malaysia.

ALAN *(Laughs)* I'm glad. *(Crosby reacts)* It means I can help you. Here's a thousand pounds to be getting on with, *(Hands over Piers's money)* get yourself a decent suit, and, oh what the hell, you can have my emergency Valentine card too.

CROSBY Thanks Alan. Hope she doesn't mind the red roses. It's the sort of thing you could send to Neil Kinnock.

ALAN *(Notes Crosby's potentially self-incriminating words)* Believe me, Vic, she'll love it. Go on, get your pen.

Crosby opens his desk drawer, looks for pen. The mousetrap snaps his fingers.

CROSBY   Ohh Christ!!!

ALAN   How did that get in there? Never mind, you can use mine. *(Uncaps ball point)*

CROSBY   *(Cradling hand)* Oh, I think it's broken! I'll have to write the card with my left hand ...

ALAN   Just don't bleed on it, she'll think you're trying to impress her.

CROSBY   *(In great pain)* What should I say then, in this coded message?

ALAN   I don't know, can't you think of something personal?

CROSBY   It's all I can do not to pass out! What did you write?

ALAN   'To Margaret from your big boy on the backbenches.'

CROSBY   And she'll know it's from you?

ALAN   She'll know it's not from Colin Moynihan. I know, why not write 'From your newest recruit.'?

Alan opens the card and places it for Crosby on Piers's blotter. Crosby writes 'From your newest recruit', then seals the envelope.

CROSBY   I'll pop it in her cubbyhole!

ALAN   We all live in hope.

Victor leaves. Alan removes the sheet of blotting paper. Beneath it is a sheet of carbon paper. He lifts that. Beneath is a sheet of House of Commons paper bearing the words 'From your newest recruit'. Alan gets the papers he took from Sir Greville's red box, puts them in an envelope with Crosby's message, seals the envelope. On the envelope already is Kinnock's name, cut out of a newspaper.

10. INT. COMMONS CHAMBER. DAY.

Early evening, day four. The Commons is sparsely attended as usual, a couple of frontbenchers and a handful of backbench extras, including Alan and Piers. Alan doesn't seem to be paying attention. He has a miniature cassette tape editing kit − and he

*is editing one cassette onto another cassette, and then listening to
the results through earphones. Meanwhile, Kinnock is on his feet
in full Welsh spate. We see him from behind.*

KINNOCK   ... These papers come from the red box of a
senior Cabinet Minister, and they clearly show price fixing
collusion between the Government and big business! I have
promised not to reveal the informer's name ... *(Alan leads
Tory shouts of 'Name him, name him')* but when I publish this
scurrilous correspondence, I'm sure the Prime Minister will
waste no time in substituting a witch hunt to track him ... or
her down. *(Sits smugly)*

11. INT. ALAN'S OFFICE. DAY.

*Day eight. Piers is telling Alan and Crosby of the grilling he's
just had in the Whips' office. Piers is standing. Alan and Crosby
sit at desks.*

PIERS   ... And then the Chief Whip shone this really bright
light into my eyes and made me tell him everything I know ...

ALAN   I thought you weren't gone long. You must be shat-
tered. If there was a spare chair you could sit down.

PIERS   Haven't they grilled you yet, Crosby?

CROSBY   Me?! I'm way above suspicion! Sir Greville looks
upon me as a son.

*Then the door bursts open and an angry taut-faced Sir Greville
enters, with a House of Commons policeman in tow.*

SIR GREVILLE   Clear your desk, Crosby!

PIERS   Congratulations Crosby! That must be the quickest
promotion since ...

SIR GREVILLE   Shut up, Fletcher Dervish, you cretin!

CROSBY   What's up?

SIR GREVILLE   You traitorous working-class worm! To think I
took you into my confidence, and how do you repay me? By
stealing papers out of my red box!

CROSBY I don't understand! Alan, you're my friend, say something!

ALAN Your friend!? You two-faced turncoat! And to think we nearly let you infiltrate this noble old party . . .

SIR GREVILLE I've misjudged you B'Stard . . .

ALAN *(Modestly)* Many do . . .

SIR GREVILLE Without your help we'd never have trapped him.

Sir Greville takes a little tape recorder from his pocket, puts it on a desk and presses play. We hear Crosby's voice, as edited by Alan.

CROSBY *(Voice on tape)* 'Yes, I admit it, I do need money, and it's the sort of thing you could send to Neil Kinnock for a thousand pounds . . .'

SIR GREVILLE *(Switches off tape)* If B'Stard hadn't managed to tape your treacherous phone call . . .

CROSBY No, no, he's faked it . . . !

SIR GREVILLE And what about the thousand pounds? Constable?

The policeman roughly takes Crosby's wallet from his inside jacket pocket, and gives it to Sir Greville, who opens it to find the bulk of the thousand pounds Alan gave him.

SIR GREVILLE Well?

CROSBY It was a gift from B'Stard . . .

SIR GREVILLE *(Pocketing money)* B'Stard's never given anyone a gift in his life! Yes, the tape was the first clue, then we compared your handwriting with the anonymous note you sent Kinnock − 'From your newest recruit'!

PIERS Crosby how could you?

SIR GREVILLE It fooled us at first, you'd obviously written it with your left hand, but our experts . . .

CROSBY *(Desperate)* No, that was on my Valentine card to Mrs Thatcher, you can check . . .

ALAN Don't be fatuous, fatso, no-one sends Maggie Valentine cards, it's common knowledge she's got no time for ridiculous things like love and romance!

SIR GREVILLE   Get him out of my sight, Constable!

The policeman hauls Crosby off. Alan immediately settles himself behind his old desk.

SIR GREVILLE   *(About to leave)* B'Stard, you've performed a noble service for the party. There could be a gong in this for you.

PIERS   Alan, I think he's inviting you to dinner.

ALAN   I don't want a knighthood . . .

SIR GREVILLE   She was thinking more of an MBE . . .

ALAN   An MBE?! That's the sort of thing you give to people like Gazza! But there's something I can offer you . . .

SIR GREVILLE   What? *(Alan produces Sir Greville's spectacles)* Oh, thank you, you found them . . . Where?

ALAN   A certain bathroom in Chelsea you no longer visit . . .

SIR GREVILLE   Oh, I see . . . all right. *(Reaches out for glasses)*

ALAN   *(Withdraws glasses)* There is a finder's fee of course, in consideration for not telling your wife where I found them . . .

SIR GREVILLE   Understood . . .

Sir Greville takes out his wallet and gives Alan the wad of money that started on Piers's desk. Alan hands the glasses to Sir Greville, crunching them in his fist as he does so.

SIR GREVILLE   *(Highly irritated)* Thank you. *(Sir Greville takes the broken spectacles and leaves)*

PIERS   I didn't understand any of that Alan.

ALAN   Of course you didn't, Piers.

Alan picks up his cordless phone and dials a number.

ALAN   *Sunday Express?* Editor please – Alan B'Stard . . . Hello, I'm afraid Victor Crosby won't be able to meet your deadline now, but I think you'll find my thoughts are quite radical . . . Okay, 'Towards a New Economic Miracle – the Case for Slavery by Alan B'Stard, indisputably the most right-wing Member of Parliament . . . '

The Party's Over

1. INT. SIR GREVILLE'S OFFICE. DAY.

A very agitated Sir Greville paces his carpet, puffing on a cigarette. Alan hurries in.

ALAN   You wanted to see me, Minister? If it's about the Stonehenge Shopping Centre planning permission, your cheque's in the post . . .

SIR GREVILLE   *(Hisses)* Shut up, B'Stard!

ALAN   What's happened? Has the Government Auditor found out about your nodding through those Iraqi export licences?

SIR GREVILLE   *(Very angry, grabs Alan's lapels. Alan is not used to being manhandled)* B'Stard, I thought they were tins of baked beans!

ALAN   Don't be stupid, baked beans tins don't normally carry directions to pull out pin, count to fifteen, and lob towards enemy . . . in Arabic.

SIR GREVILLE   It doesn't matter. What I have to speak to you about is far more important. I'm talking about total financial ruin for the entire country!

Sir Greville sits behind his desk, stubs out his cigarette and takes another from box on desk. Alan picks up the silver table lighter, lights Sir Greville's cigarette.

SIR GREVILLE B'Stard, what has been the lynchpin of Tory success since 1979?

ALAN A gullible electorate? A tame press? General Galtieri? Neil Kinnock?

SIR GREVILLE North Sea oil. Our tax cuts, our unemployment hand-outs, they've all been subsidised by North Sea oil. Have you heard of Professor Eugene Quail?

ALAN The Government Chief Scientific Advisor?

SIR GREVILLE Yes.

ALAN Never heard of him.

SIR GREVILLE This morning he came to Cabinet and told us the oil is running out.

ALAN Nothing lasts for ever. Not even sex with me.

SIR GREVILLE The oil won't even last that long! We thought we would be self-sufficient in oil until about 2015, but last week Quail double-checked the figures, and we've only got a teaspoon of the stuff left!

ALAN So when the computer said 2015 it actually meant quarter past eight?! Why is he still working for the Government? Why don't you deport him?

SIR GREVILLE He knows too much.

ALAN He knows bugger all about oil.

SIR GREVILLE It isn't his fault. It seems the figures were tampered with by someone at Number Ten, someone very important . . .

ALAN Someone who now lives in Dulwich?

SIR GREVILLE I'm afraid so. Apparently they only discovered the computer disc with the real information when the builders knocked down the partition wall between her bed and Denis's . . . *(Runs hand through hair. He really is in a state)* There's going to be a slump that'll make the crash of 1929 look like the first day of Harrods' sale. We're projecting output down by fifty percent, unemployment up to ten million, food riots, national strikes, blood in the gutters . . .

ALAN Bad news for anyone who hadn't the foresight to buy a holiday home in the West Indies . . .

SIR GREVILLE So we've decided to go to the country as soon as possible, win a snap election, then batten down the hatches until the fiscal storm blows over.

ALAN Why are you telling me this? I suppose you want me to put a big bet on Labour for you?

SIR GREVILLE I'm telling you because the Galloping Major wants you to master-mind our election campaign.

ALAN What?! Why me?!

SIR GREVILLE Because you're energetic, radical, charismatic . . .

ALAN Especially compared to the PM . . .

SIR GREVILLE And since your guest appearance on *Coronation Street*, you're the best known Conservative in the country.

ALAN Of course . . . But then the Cabinet's so anonymous, all bar Tarzan could go on *What's My Line* and the panel wouldn't stand a chance. Though the mime might be a giveaway. *(Mimes wanking)*

SIR GREVILLE   So, will you do it?

ALAN   If the man on the flying trapeze thinks I'm the chap for the job, then I'll give it a go. After all, the eighties have been good to me, and this is my chance to put something back . . .

SIR GREVILLE   Excellent, then you can start with my table lighter.

ALAN   What?! *(Puts hand in pocket and comes up with table lighter)* Thank God, I thought I had a growth!

2. INT. ALAN'S OFFICE. DAY.

Day one — a couple of days later. Alan and Piers are putting up wall charts, posters, and generally turning the office into an election campaign centre. Lots of action through first half of this scene.

PIERS   I love elections. I got ever so excited at the leadership ballot . . .

ALAN   I remember the mess . . . You never did tell me who you voted for . . .

PIERS   I voted for Mrs Thatcher of course.

ALAN   And in the second ballot?

PIERS   What second ballot?

ALAN   Piers, have you any idea who the new Prime Minister actually is?

PIERS   Of course, he's . . . a tall grey-haired chap . . . er, hang on, yes, it's Major Michael Douglas, you know, the actor . . .

ALAN   And you'd do anything to help get Major Douglas re-elected?

PIERS   Anything, Alan.

ALAN   Good, because an unusual mind like yours is perfect for the glamorous world of media manipulation. So I want you to set up an advertising agency.

PIERS   But I don't know anything about advertising.

ALAN   You don't know anything about politics, but you work here. It'll be easy. I'll write all the commercials myself, you just sign the large imaginative invoices I draw up, and I keep the money.

PIERS   But what's in it for me?

ALAN   That's typical of your nasty, grasping Thatcherite attitude, Piers. I've just introduced you into the glamorous jet set world of advertising! Are you never satisfied?

PIERS   Sorry Alan.

ALAN   I should think so.

PIERS   Alan, now that I'm in advertising, I've had a fantastic idea for a Tory Party election poster. A big picture of the Prime Minister and underneath the words 'Vote Conservative . . . please'.

ALAN   No, too sophisticated. It presupposes the electorate can handle complex abstract concepts, like 'vote'. No, I think we have to appeal to the essential heart of the British character.

PIERS   You mean offer them strong leadership and prudent financial management?

ALAN   No, offer them four free cans of lager and the chance to win a weekend with Gazza. And for the middle classes, free Marks and Spencer Chicken Granthams.

PIERS   What's Chicken Grantham?

ALAN   It's a new range in honour of Lady Thatcher of Suburbia. They're like Chicken Kiev, but when you cut them open there's bugger all inside.

PIERS   But that's dishonest, Alan!

ALAN   There is no alternative, Piers. Sir Greville turned down my other suggestion.

PIERS   What was that?

ALAN   Rounding up known Labour supporters in marginal constituencies and holding them until the election's over.

PIERS   That's awful, you can't do that!

ALAN   *(Regretfully)* No . . .

PIERS   Thank God.

ALAN   That's how we won in 1987 and Sir Greville doesn't think we'd get away with it twice.

PIERS   How would you find out who voted Labour?

ALAN   There's a serial number on every ballot paper, everyone
        knows that.

PIERS   So you could find out I voted Labour . . . for example?

ALAN   What do you mean?

PIERS   I was just being hypothetical.

ALAN   *(Threateningly)* No you weren't! You did vote Labour,
        didn't you?

PIERS   There were lots of candidates, I got confused.

ALAN   You were voting in your own constituency! Your name
        was on the ballot paper!

PIERS   Sorry Alan . . .

ALAN   I'm going to have to help you remember who to vote for next time, Piers . . .

Picks up Piers's monogrammed seal and sealing wax from Piers's desk, lights a match, drips hot wax on the back of Piers's hand and stamps Piers's seal down on it. Piers screams in agony.

ALAN   There, you should be all right now, as long as there isn't another candidate with the same initials.

The screen goes blank. A voice over says

VOICE OVER   There now follows a party political broadcast on behalf of the Conservative Party, by Alan B'Stard MP, deputy chairman of the Conservative Party.

3. INT. TV STUDIO. NIGHT.

On the television screens in our homes we see the famous bit of footage of Gazza crying at the World Cup. Freeze frame and mix into a TV presentation studio, where Alan sits behind a desk, looking sincere and gorgeous.

ALAN   Good evening. Who in this country was not moved when that great Englishman, Gazza, wept bitter tears at the World Cup last year? People thought he was crying because he had just been booked by the referee, and so would miss the final. But that was not the reason. He was crying at the thought that the Conservative Government, the only government this young hero had ever known, was behind in the opinion polls. He was weeping at the threat of the return to power of a Labour rabble led by a bald, Welsh windbag, dedicated to destroying our prosperity, giving power back to trades union dictators, running down our currency, encouraging satanist abuse of our children, spreading Aids through their sponsorship of homosexual behaviour, abolishing the House of Lords, and executing the royal family. Gazza didn't want that for his children. Do you want it for yours? Or do you want a government that lets you share in

Britain's prosperity by offering you the chance of five, yes five, free Sun jackpot bingo cards with every registered Tory membership application? *(Produces a fan of bingo cards to camera)* Yes, apply now to join the Tory Party at this week's once in a lifetime, special offer price of only nine ninety nine, and you will receive a free Tarzan Teenage Hero Turtle T-shirt, a Gazza car tidy, free entry for a family of four to the Haltemprice Safari Park, and the *News of the World* every

Sunday for a year. But don't join the Tories simply because we're the value for money party; join us because we're right. Listen to what young Britons have to say.

We see two rough-voiced lager louts — Union Jack T-shirts and tattoos.

LOUT 1   I vote Conservative because only the Conservatives can defend this country's sovereignty in the face of Jacques Delors's expansionism.

LOUT 2   Yeah, I mean, if we get a Central European Bank in Germany or something, then how's our government going to keep its hands on the main levers of fiscal policy — namely interest rates, money supply and public expenditure. Right?

We return to studio, Alan is behind his desk as before.

ALAN   And what about working women? What are the Tories doing for them?

Widen shot to see Alan is flanked by two gorgeous pouting Star *birds in tight* Star *T-shirts.*

STAR BIRD   Labour claim to be the party of feminism, but only the sound fiscal policies of the Tories can create a climate in which the labour force continues to expand and job opportunities increase.

ALAN   Well, there you have it . . . well I certainly did. Ordinary young people, picked at random. They're going to vote Tory. Are you? Or are you really stupid? Goodnight.

4. INT. ALAN'S OFFICE. DAY.

A couple of weeks later. Alan's office is full of election material. The display board shows the Tories are now well in the lead. As well as bar graphs for the main parties, there is a tall column marked L.S.D.. Alan is opening his fan mail. He reads one aloud.

ALAN   'Dear Alan B'Stard, I just had to write to say you're bloody great. I've had a gizzard full of lefties telling us we ought to look after the less well off. Bugger them! I'm with you Al. Magic. All the best, Melvin Bragg.'

The door opens and Piers makes an entrance. He has turned into an advertising executive: oversized Paul Smith suit, floral bow tie, big red-rimmed glasses, gelled hair, mobile phone, and matt black, rubberised briefcase.

PIERS   Hi A.B. *(Piers sits in his revolving chair, puts his feet up on the desk. Alan spins the chair very fast)* Aaah!

ALAN   Where do you think you've been?!

PIERS   *(Slowing down)* The Groucho Club, power lunching.

ALAN   Who with? You don't know anyone powerful except me.

PIERS   That's where you're wrong. I've just done a deal with the owner of the biggest chain of poster sites in the South.

ALAN   *(Almost impressed)* Biggest in the South?

PIERS   I knew you'd be impressed. It wasn't easy, and it wasn't cheap, but by the end of the week our posters will be all over Dublin.

ALAN   Piers, come here . . . *(Takes Piers by the ear and leads him to the wall map)*

PIERS   Aah! ow!

ALAN   *(Bangs Piers's face into map)* Dublin is not in the United Kingdom!

PIERS   No?! Since when?

Sir Greville enters. He looks very serious, and smokes nervily. Alan pushes Piers away.

ALAN   Sir Greville! Welcome to the war room. *(Points to board)* Eleven points ahead, we can call the election any time we like, we'll romp it!

PIERS   Perhaps we should call it the romper room, Alan.

SIR GREVILLE   What's he doing here?! And why is he dressed like a breakfast television astrologer?

ALAN   Piers is in charge of media. The perfect choice, being mediocre.

SIR GREVILLE   Then send the dolt out to buy a comic, I have to speak to you in private.

Piers looks at Alan, then shoots out.

ALAN   If it's about the vicious rumours that I've been creaming money off the campaign fund . . . ?

SIR GREVILLE   Of course you have, B'Stard, we'd worry if you didn't. But what's more important is that the opposition parties are in total disarray. We're heading for a landslide!

ALAN   *(Modest)* I just talk to the great British public in their own language: fluent Greed.

SIR GREVILLE   *(Sighs deeply)* I wanted to confide in you from the start, but Major wasn't having any . . .

ALAN   Yes, he does look rather frustrated round the upper lip. Confide what in me?

SIR GREVILLE   We don't *want* to win the election! Not with total economic collapse around the corner! The whole idea of appointing you was that you'd run such an odious campaign the public would all vote Labour. Then *they'd* have to carry the can . . . !

ALAN   *(Taken aback)* Oh! Then you over-estimated the sensitivity of the average British voter. Why didn't you tell me we were supposed to lose?!

PIERS   *(Re-enters)* Excuse me, Alan, what comic did you want me to buy?

ALAN   Who cares! *Beano, Dandy, Daily Express,* just go! No, wait a minute . . . *(Alan has had a brill idea)* Piers, Sir Greville and I have some very exciting news for you.

PIERS   You have?

SIR GREVILLE   We have?

ALAN   Yes. After your success in carrying the poster campaign beyond mere national boundaries, we've decided to put *you* in charge of our entire election effort.

Alan shakes Piers's bandaged hand. Piers whimpers.

5. INT. COMMONS SMOKING ROOM. NIGHT.

A week later. Open on tight close-up on the television in the corner of the smoking room. Someone is interviewing a power-dressed Piers on News at Ten, *about his new Tory Party campaign.*

INTERVIEWER ... This new poster campaign is certainly very different from last month's Tory Party giveaway bonanza?

PIERS Well, I thought I would try to reflect the new spirit of the caring nineties and bring a little, you know, honesty and modesty into political advertising ...

Widen to see Alan is watching the TV, with large brandy in hand. The smoking room is empty save for an old MP who snoozes in an armchair throughout the scene, with a copy of The Guardian *over his face.*

ALAN Well memorised, Piers.

PIERS After all, no party can be right all the time, can it?

INTERVIEWER *(Taken aback)* No, indeed not. Let's take a look at Piers Fletcher Dervish's controversial new advertisements.

On the screen we see three examples of Piers's new posters. They consist of bold blue lettering on a white background.

'We're responsible for this mess, you ought to let us clear it up. Vote Conservative.'

'Poll tax was a dreadful mistake, and we'd like to get rid of it, but we can't think of anything to put in its place so let's try to make the best of it. Vote Conservative.'

PIERS This is my special favourite ... *(Reads next poster as we see it)*

'Mrs Thatcher may have gone, but don't worry, behind the scenes she's still running the country.'

ALAN *(Delighted, he raises his brandy glass to the screen)* Piers, you're a genius.

Paddy O'Rourke, Labour bigwig, suddenly strides into the smoking room, and pulls the TV plug out of the wall.

PADDY O'ROURKE   All right, B'Stard, what are you up to? We're fifteen points ahead in the polls!

ALAN   Yes, it does look as if a Labour victory is assured.

PADDY O'ROURKE   What the hell is going on?!

ALAN   *(Takes out and consults diary)* Well, there's the House of Lords Annual Mass Pacemaker Recharging . . .

PADDY O'ROURKE   You know damn well what I mean! Why are you trying to lose the election?!

ALAN   Me? I'm Mr Win At Any Price! *(A steward comes over)* Two brandies, one Napoleon, one cooking. *(Steward goes)*

PADDY O'ROURKE   Then why have you put a man with a bath sponge for a brain in charge of the campaign? There's some catastrophe on the horizon, isn't there? And you Tories don't want to be in power when it happens, do you? You've got to tell me, B'Stard!

ALAN   All right, listen. *(Beat)* Oil.

PADDY O'ROURKE   Oil? What about it?

ALAN   It's running out. By the end of the year our only oil reserves will be in Kenneth Baker's hair.

PADDY O'ROURKE   Of course! So you want *us* to form the next government! You want *us* to have to deal with the total collapse of British industry, go cap in hand to the Common Market for emergency aid, beg the German Bundesbank to take over the running of the economy leading to a nationalist backlash that will sweep us from power into the gutter of history, and bring you back just as we get the crisis under control!

ALAN   Yes. It's an old trick, but what do you expect with a circus performer as PM? Now about my fee . . .

PADDY O'ROURKE   Fee!? Why should I pay you anything now you've told me?

ALAN   Because I haven't told you *how* you can avoid forming the next government.

PADDY O'ROURKE   *(Eagerly)* How?

Steward brings the drinks, one in a large balloon, the other in a small shot glass. Paddy looks pained but accepts his meagre drink. Steward goes.

PADDY O'ROURKE   *(Quieter)* How?

ALAN   Please, Paddy, money first ... And not the usual Labour Party petty cash, please.

PADDY O'ROURKE   We haven't got ...

ALAN   Don't give me that, I happen to know you've had an offer from someone who wants to buy Labour Party headquarters to turn it into a private hospital.

PADDY O'ROURKE   We'd never sell! Besides, it was a derisory offer!

ALAN   *(Knowingly)* It's the best you're going to get ...

PADDY O'ROURKE   *(Knows when he's licked)* All right, I'll talk to Glynis ... *(Gets up to go)*

ALAN   Before you leave, Paddy, have you ever wondered why they call this the Smoking Room?

Alan gets out his lighter and sets fire to the paper covering the sleeping MP. Alan goes off laughing. Paddy beats the fire out with a cushion as the old member sleeps on.

6. INT. COMMONS CHAMBER. DAY.

A week later. Mid-afternoon. The chamber is quite full. Alan and Piers on the backbench. Paddy O'Rourke is on his feet introducing the new Labour Party policy document 'Spend now, worry later'.

PADDY O'ROURKE   ...Of course, the Government will attempt to slash expenditure in the face of this oil crisis, and so turn recession into depression. But we in the Labour Party believe we must expand and borrow our way out of this downturn, and so I am proud to be the author of our new policy document 'Spend Now, Worry Later'. *(Tory jeers)* If elected we will double old age pensions, eliminate health service waiting lists, and abolish value-added tax. We cost

these proposals at seven hundred billion pounds in a full year
. . .

ALAN   *(Jumping to his feet)* And how are you going to pay for all this?

PADDY O'ROURKE   Ah, there the Honourable Member for Haltemprice has hit upon the one small problem in this exciting new manifesto. *(Sits. Uproar in House)*

PIERS   *(Confused)* I don't understand, Alan. What's he doing?

ALAN   Emulating you, Piers, telling the truth about his Party's policy.

PIERS   But then no one will vote Labour! Even I can see that's being silly.

ALAN   Then the Liberals can take power and put their half-baked fantasies into effect . . .

A Liberal stands.

LIBERAL   I should just like to say on behalf of the Liberal Democrats that though we are very nice people, we don't actually have any idea how to run the country. *(Sits)*

7. INT. ALAN'S OFFICE. NIGHT.

An hour later. Alan is adjusting the bar graphs on his chart. The L.S.D. — Alan's financial position — is streaking away with the election. It will soon be off the chart and on to the wall. Piers rushes in with the early editions of the next day's papers which he puts down on Alan's desk.

PIERS   Alan, have you seen the *Telegraph* poll?,

ALAN   Why, have you lost one?

PIERS   No, I mean *The Daily Telegraph*. They've carried out a phone survey of voting intentions now everyone knows the oil's running out. Look, Tories four per cent, Labour four per cent, Liberals four per cent, 'Do Not Intend To Vote' seventy-seven per cent . . . The only parties holding their own are the Ulster Unionists and Sinn Fein. Suppose they form a coalition?

ALAN That's about as likely as Prince Charles putting in aluminium replacement windows at Kensington Palace.

PIERS Then what's going to happen, Alan?!

ALAN *(Arm round Piers's shoulder)* What's going to happen is that people who keep their nerve will make a killing!

PIERS Oh no Alan, I draw the line at murder!

ALAN A stock market killing! Tell me, are you a bull, a bear, or a stag?

PIERS I don't know, Alan, but Clarissa calls me her little beaver hound!

ALAN *(Pulls a disgusted face)* Look, do you want a really hot stock market tip or not?

PIERS *(Eagerly)* Yes?

ALAN It's not free!

PIERS Sorry, Alan. *(Takes out cheque book)* How much?

ALAN Just sign a few blank ones. *(Piers does so)* All right, buy oil, you'll make a killing. *(The phone rings)* Go on, answer it. You know what to say.

PIERS *(Tough guy)* Hello, no, Mr B'Stard's far too busy to waste his time with the likes of you! *(Hangs up)*

ALAN Excellent, Piers. And if you spoke to your constituents like that, you'd have more time to make money too.

PIERS Oh, it wasn't a constituent, it was Sir Greville.

ALAN Shit! *(Dashes out)*

8. INT. SIR GREVILLE'S OFFICE. NIGHT.

A few minutes later. A depressed and tired Sir Greville sits at his desk. He smokes a cigarette, unaware that another smoulders in the ash tray.

SIR GREVILLE B'Stard, is Fletcher Dervish completely insane?

ALAN Yes.

SIR GREVILLE Thought so. I think I might be cracking up myself. My share portfolio's about to go through the floor, my house is going to be worth slightly less than it was when it was built in 1763, we're neck and neck with Labour again . . .

ALAN   At four per cent each it's more ankle and ankle . . .

SIR GREVILLE   It's all because of this blasted oil leak! What am I going to do?!

ALAN   I use a very good little garage in Pimlico.

SIR GREVILLE   Major suspects *me*! I've got to find the culprit! You haven't been talking to your filthy Fleet Street friends, have you?

ALAN   Of course not.

SIR GREVILLE   Well everyone knows!

ALAN   How?

SIR GREVILLE   *(Flash of paranoia)* Of course! Howe! Just Geoffrey's style! Bitter old has-been! *(Regains control)* No, calm down Greville, don't lose it now . . .

ALAN   I bet you'd give anything for things to be the way they were before all this blew up?

SIR GREVILLE   Anything, anything!

ALAN   Well, I do have an idea, it's a desperate throw, it won't be cheap, and I may not come out of it alive . . .

SIR GREVILLE   You owe it to Britain.

ALAN   I'm going to dictate a letter. *(Sir Greville uncaps pen)* To the Governor of the Bank of England, this letter introduces my friend Alan B'Stard, who is on urgent Government business. He will have a large sack with him. Help him fill it . . .

Mix through to

9. INT. CORRIDOR. NIGHT.

A minute later. Alan comes out of Sir Greville's office holding the letter. He kisses it, then takes a small cellular phone from his pocket and presses one of the pre-sets.

ALAN   Professor Quail, please . . . Believe me, he'll want to be woken up . . . Hello, Eugene? Time to tell the world you've made a ghastly mistake.

10. INT. ALAN'S OFFICE. DAY.

The next day, Alan is stuffing wads of money into his desk. Every drawer is full of money. Eventually he has a wad left over. On the wall chart the money column is well off the chart and up the wall. Alan half considers throwing the odd wad out of the window. Throughout this, the early evening news is on television. Professor Quail is making a statement.

PROF. QUAIL . . . I made a ghastly mistake. I grossly underestimated Britain's North Sea oil reserves, and I have already tendered my resignation.

Newsreader returns to TV screen.

NEWSREADER Oil shares bounced back in the aftermath of Professor Quail's statement, which has abruptly ended the recent bout of election fever . . .

Piers enters glumly, kicks a chair. Alan zaps off the TV.

ALAN What's wrong, Piers? Didn't you take my advice about buying oil?

PIERS Yes I took it, and now Clarissa's livid! I've got two thousand cases of Mazola stored in the garage and she can't get her bike out. And she says fried food's bad for me . . . !

ALAN *(Chuckles)* Piers, wallet.

PIERS Oh, Alan!

ALAN Wallet! *(Piers reluctantly gives Alan his wallet. Alan takes the wad of cash from his desktop and crams them into Piers's wallet)* These are the caring nineties. Go and have some fun, Piers.

PIERS Oh, money for me . . . ? *(His brain cannot cope with the enormity of Alan's action. He faints)*

There is a knock on the door and Quail enters.

ALAN Eugene, you don't look like a man who has just lost his job, his reputation, his pension plan . . .

PROF. QUAIL Yes, I'm heart-broken. I have a wife, three children, a mortgage . . .

ALAN *(Passing him a large well-stuffed brown envelope)* . . . A million pounds for helping bring off the biggest stock market scam this century ...

PROF. QUAIL　Yes, and to think I was a struggling civil servant ...

ALAN　... Until the day I spotted you coming out of that transvestite nightclub ...

PROF. QUAIL　I must be the first person to make a profit out of being blackmailed.

ALAN　Well, these are the caring nineties, Eugene. *(Slaps him*

on the back heartily. Feels the fabric of his under garment) Oh, real silk?

PROF. QUAIL	*(Proud)* Janet Reger.

ALAN	Nice.

Natural Selection

1. INT. HALTEMPRICE DRAWING ROOM. NIGHT.

A cocktail party for local Tory bigwigs is taking place in Alan's northern headquarters. A waiter circulates with drinks tray. A palm court trio plays arthritically. Piers is present, chatting with a group of people. Also among the guests are Ken Price, a blunt but not unsophisticated local builder of about forty-five, and his twenty-three-year-old fiancée, Cher Titley, very pretty, but rather naïve. The door to the kitchen is half open, and we glimpse Mr and Mrs B'Stard, doing it doggy style on the kitchen table. We hear Alan's grunts as he reaches the moment of truth. Then we see that Sarah, bent forward over the table, has one eye on a saucepan boiling on the hob, and the other on a cook book on stand in front of her. Alan pulls out and pulls up his half-mast trousers.

SARAH   Has anyone ever told you you're the perfect lover?

ALAN   Madonna mumbled something of the sort, but she had her mouth full at the time . . .

SARAH   *(Crosses to hob, takes pan off the boil)* There can't be many men you can use to time a pan of soft-boiled quails' eggs. Fifty-five seconds. Perfect.

ALAN   *(Proudly)* Nearly a minute, eh?

Sarah crosses to sink to shell the eggs. Alan adjusts his clothes.

ALAN   I suppose I'd better go and mingle now with the pathetic polyester-clad peasants cluttering up my drawing room.

SARAH   Alan, they're your constituents! And some of them are my friends!

ALAN   That doesn't excuse all those man-made fibres. Every time I shake hands I'll get a static shock. Why have you invited them here anyway?

SARAH   To meet you! It's so long since you've been seen in Haltemprice, people are starting to think you've become Terry Waite's room-mate. You're supposed to advise and help your constituents . . .

ALAN   I'd willingly help them, but euthanasia is illegal in this country.

SARAH   *(Wheedling)* I know one constituent with a really big problem that you could solve with a stroke of your pen.

ALAN   Sarah, for the last time, I am not spending three hundred thousand pounds on an indoor equestrian centre.

SARAH   But darling . . .

ALAN   I know you, you'll only use it once, like that ocean-going yacht you made me waste a million on. What happened to that?

SARAH   It ran out of petrol.

ALAN   I'm so sorry. Next time I'll buy you a supertanker!

SARAH   Anyway you didn't really buy the yacht for me, you bought it to run guns into West Beirut.

ALAN   Who told you that?!

SARAH   The five swarthy terrorists I found lounging around the state room last time I went on board.

ALAN   *(Cynical)* I'm sure you all got on very well.

SARAH   Very well indeed. *(Dreamy)* If I ever need to time a pan of hard-boiled ostrich eggs . . .

Sarah now has shelled and halved the quails' eggs and put them in a dish. Piers knocks on the door and enters.

PIERS   *(Urgently)* Alan, listen, you know there's going to be an election within the next eighteen months!?

ALAN   No, really!? Better phone the papers straight away!

PIERS   Oh, righty ho . . .

Off he goes. Alan, Sarah, and the eggs enter the main room. Guests cluster round. Alan looks disdainfully at them. He takes a small aerosol air freshener from a pocket and sprays the crowd. Then he spots Cher Titley across the room and decides to make for her. Meanwhile, Sarah rather likes the look of Ken Price, and eases away from Alan towards him. Several constituents try to talk to Alan as he moves towards Cher. The first is an elderly man.

ELDERLY MAN   Mr B'Stard, what are you going to do about that awful Do It All they're building bang in the middle of our beautiful village of Edgworthy?

ALAN   What am I going to do? I'm going to make five million pounds, I own the land. *(Pushes the old man away)*

Then a rather spotty young woman grabs Alan's arm. Alan shakes her off.

YOUNG WOMAN   Mr B'Stard, would it be too dreadfully impolite for me to ask you why you haven't held a single surgery since 1988?!

ALAN   *(Grimaces)* No more impolite than it would be for me to remark that your skin makes General Noriega look like Katie Boyle, and your breath would disgrace a woolly mammoth that had just been thawed out after twenty thousand years beneath the Siberian Tundra, and whose last meal before the onset of the ice age was five tons of garlic. *(Young woman looks horrified)* Now when you tell your friends you've never been so insulted, you'll be telling the truth.

Alan moves towards Cher again. In the background Sarah is chatting up Ken Price. Piers re-appears.

PIERS   Alan, Alan, you know you're MP for Haltemprice . . . !?

ALAN   Am I really, Piers? I wondered why I have a House of

Commons car park sticker on my Rolls ... *(Sees waiter passing, snaps fingers)* Champagne cocktail, Piers.

Piers gets him one, and Alan throws it over Piers. Piers goes off looking for a towel. Alan takes two more cocktails from waiter and finally reaches Cher.

ALAN　*(Gives her drink)* Hello. I of course am Alan B'Stard, and you are the only woman in this room who doesn't look like a failed experiment by Dr Frankenstein. Tell me your name.

CHER TITLEY　Cher ...

ALAN　Cher ... so you must be named after the singer, film star and plastic surgery addict?

Cher giggles. Piers comes back for one last try, interrupting Alan's flow.

PIERS　Alan, Alan, can you see that man talking to Sarah?!

ALAN　I can. *(Pokes Piers in eye with cocktail stick)* But you can't, can you?

Piers screams in agony and falls to the floor. Alan takes Cher by the elbow and treads on Piers as he leads Cher across the room to a sofa where they sit. We focus on Sarah and Price.

KEN PRICE Three hundred grand?! I'd build your equestrian centre for two hundred thousand, cash. And I know where you can get a good stallion to go with it.

SARAH You'd really put it up for me?

KEN PRICE Just ask!

SARAH And how long would it take?

KEN PRICE As long as you like, Mrs B'Stard.

SARAH Call me Sarah.

KEN PRICE I'll call you tomorrow.

SARAH Mr Price, I thought you were engaged to be married?

KEN PRICE I am. She's a lovely innocent lass, but you and me are people of the world, and a little discreet liaison . . . *(Then he spots Alan getting on well with Cher)* What's she doing talking to him?!

Ken Price strides across to confront Alan. On his way he knocks over Piers again as he struggles to his feet.

KEN PRICE What the hell do you think you're at, B'Stard?

ALAN Do you mind, I'm talking to this delectable young lady.

KEN PRICE That's my bloody fiancée!

ALAN Then you should be gratified that someone as important and influential as me has time to waste on the betrothed of a nonentity. *(To Cher)* Who is he anyway?

KEN PRICE I'm Ken Price, and you'd know who I am if you spent more than five minutes a year in your bloody constituency.

ALAN Five minutes a year is too long with loudmouthed babysnatchers like you living here!

KEN PRICE At least I live in the constituency! At least I know my way around Haltemprice without a guide dog. At least my business is based in Yorkshire, and benefits Yorkshire!

ALAN Don't tell me, you own a flourishing chain of tripe shops!

KEN PRICE   I own Pricerite Builders, the biggest housebuilders in the North.

ALAN   So *you* built the estate of vile little stack-a-pleb maisonettes that's ruined my view across the moors?

KEN PRICE   Affordable homes for tomorrow's families!

ALAN   Until they've saved the money for something more substantial, like a cardboard box!

KEN PRICE   Listen chum, you'll be laughing the other side of your smarmy face when Pricerite Builders goes public next week, and I bank fifty million pounds!

ALAN   Going public!? *(To Cher)* In that case, you can't possibly marry him, Cher!

CHER TITLEY   Why not?

ALAN   Because it'll make you Cher Price. Do you want people in the City gossiping about his share price going down?

Cher giggles. Ken punches Alan hard in the mouth. Alan falls to the floor.

KEN PRICE   Now people can talk about the ex-MP for Haltemprice going down!

ALAN   *(Stunned, handkerchief to bleeding mouth)* What?!

KEN PRICE   Yes, if you ever attended a constituency executive meeting, you'd know you'd been de-selected. That's right, *I'm* going to be the next MP for Haltemprice!

The gathered constituency bigwigs all look pleased.

YOUNG WOMAN   We were wondering how to break it to you.

PIERS   *(Reappears with an eye patch)* Alan, listen, Ken Price is going to be the next MP for Haltemprice!

Alan reaches out a hand as if asking Piers to help him to his feet. As Alan rises, he manages to butt Piers in the nose with the crown of his head.

2. INT. RAILWAY CARRIAGE. DAY.

Alan and Piers are in a pair of seats at the end of a branch line guard's van. It's dirty. The cage of the guard's van holds dozens of baskets of racing pigeons, plus mail bags and other luggage. Alan has a fat lip, Piers has his eye patch and a plastered nose. Alan is on the mobile phone, while Piers has an envelope of old stamps, a magnifying glass, and a catalogue on his knees. There is a wicker basket in the aisle — a hamper prepared by Piers.

ALAN   ... Oh, very comfortable — considering we're in the guard's van — Piers booked the tickets, apparently he asked for maximum privacy ... Look, have you got any dirt on Price yet? *(Resignedly)* Yes, I'll make it worth your while ... *(The train enters a tunnel cutting Alan off)* Bugger! *(Switches phone off)* What are you doing?

PIERS   I'm just checking some stamps I bought at the Harrogate Stamp Fair yesterday ... *(Eyes widen and he becomes hysterically excited)* Haaaaaaaaaaa!!!!

ALAN   What is it?!

PIERS   Look! This one! I bought it in a mixed packet for ten pounds, and it's got two more perforations on the left-hand side than on the right!

ALAN   That will knock the Gulf crisis off the front pages.

PIERS   *(Points to catalogue)* No, don't you see, that makes it worth five thousand pounds!

ALAN   But it's used!

PIERS   Oh, Alan, you're so silly . . .

ALAN   *(Stands up and smacks the stamps off Piers's lap onto the floor)* I'm what!?

PIERS   *(Scrabbling on the floor)* Sorry Alan.

While Piers is on the floor looking for a stamp that Alan is deliberately standing on, the guard comes along. Alan points the wicker basket out to him. He picks up the basket and puts it with the baskets of pigeons, and disappears down the train. Alan moves his foot to reveal the precious stamp.

PIERS   Got it! *(Puts precious stamp in a special little leather wallet, and stands)*

ALAN   What's that?

PIERS   These are my most collectable stamps. The stamps in this little wallet are worth over half a million pounds!

ALAN   What?!

PIERS   Yes, there's one Daddy bought for pennies before the war, that's now worth over one hundred thousand pounds! And it's all tax free capital gain!

ALAN   Piers, why are you suddenly making sense?

PIERS   Julian Whitaker told me.

ALAN   What, a junior treasury minister's been giving you financial advice?

PIERS   Well, you see, we're both in the Parliamentary Stamp Club. He thought I was his friend . . . until I told him I was running against him for Stamp Club President.

ALAN   He must be terrified. After all, he's only a highly thought of ex-Balliol College economist, strongly tipped to succeed Badger Lamont as Chancellor. Whereas you're a cretin.

PIERS   Aha, Julian won't have time to write an election address as funny as mine . . .

ALAN   You mean, care of The Society for the Protection of Dickheads, Milton Keynes?

PIERS   No, I mean he'll be too busy working on the Budget. Alan, do you want to hear my best stamp joke?

ALAN   I'd rather have my penis surgically removed without anaesthetic . . . Does Whitaker ever talk about what might be in the Budget?

PIERS   Of course not, it's top secret!

ALAN   I don't know why the Budget is surrounded by such paranoia. It's always terribly predictable; twopence on beer, a penny off income tax, and ten pounds off television licences for the blind.

PIERS   Blind people are entitled to extra help.

ALAN   You wouldn't say that if David Blunkett's guide dog had dumped on *your* new hand-made suede brogues! Now if I were Chancellor the Budget would be worth listening to. For a start I'd abolish income tax, abolish social security, and give a million pounds a year to anyone whose surname starts with B apostrophe. *(Looks at watch)* Time for coffee I think.

PIERS   I'll get the hamper. *(Looks around)* Where is it?

ALAN   It was in the way, the guard put it in his cage. It's the top one on the left.

Piers opens the door of the cage and gets the hamper Alan points to. He opens it. Racing pigeons fly out. Alarmed racing pigeons. Piers tries to catch them. They dump on Piers. Alan opens the window and shoos most of them out.

ALAN   I think the game pie is a shade undercooked.

PIERS   My jacket!

Piers starts trying to clean bird droppings off with his hankie. Alan gets the proper hamper and takes out a bottle of mineral water.

ALAN   Alow me.

Alan pours the whole litre of water over Piers's jacket. Piers exclaims. Alan helps him out of the soaking garment, opens the door window and hangs the jacket from the catch. We may not notice Alan lift Piers's stamp wallet from its pocket.

ALAN   It'll soon get nice and dry here . . .

Alan 're-arranges' the jacket on its hook, so that the wind whips the jacket away. Piers gives an agonised yelp.

PIERS   My jacket!! My stamps!!

Piers sticks his head and torso out of the window of the door to see if he can spot his jacket.

PIERS   Alan, pull the communication cord!
ALAN   Don't be silly, it's a hundred pound fine!
PIERS   Sorry, I wasn't thinking.
ALAN   *(Joining Piers at the window)* Look, isn't that your jacket caught on the next carriage?

Piers peers out. As he does so, Alan gently opens the door.

PIERS   Wherrrrrrre!?

For the door swings open and Piers vanishes. Alan laughs. The train jolts. Alan nearly falls out too. He recovers, slams the door, sits down, takes a good swig from his hip flask, opens Piers's stamp wallet and starts looking up values in the catalogue.

3. INT. PRIVATE HOSPITAL ROOM. DAY.

The next day. Piers is in a hospital bed. A broken arm and a broken leg are plastered. The leg is in a hoist. His head is bandaged, his jaw is wired, and he is on a saline drip. Alan enters with a nice box of chocolates. He sees a sign above the bed that reads 'nil by mouth'.

ALAN   Nil Bymouth? You've got a Swedish doctor?
PIERS   Mff mff!
ALAN   As long as he warms his hands first, eh? You know, you

gave me a nasty turn jumping off the train . . .

PIERS (Who knows he didn't jump) Mff!

ALAN I've brought you some nice chocolates. The David Owen selection – all hard centres. Oh well . . .

Alan opens the box and has a chocolate. Then the door opens, and Julian Whitaker enters with some flowers. Whitaker is very tall, very thin, and very posh.

JULIAN WHITAKER I came as soon as I heard.

ALAN Oh, so you're into telephone sex, are you?

JULIAN WHITAKER (Smiles politely at Alan's joke) Fletcher Dervish, what actually happened?

PIERS (Accusingly at Alan) Mff mff mff!

ALAN He says he jumped off the train in despair after his prize stamps blew out of the window.

PIERS (Contradicting Alan) Mff, mff mfff mmfff!

JULIAN WHITAKER How awful. I suppose that means he won't be running for Stamp Club President now?

PIERS (Protests) Mff mff mff mff!

ALAN I don't imagine he'll be running for anything for a while. Never mind, Piers, there's always next year.

JULIAN WHITAKER No there isn't, because once I'm in power, I'm going to abolish these piffling annual Stamp Club elections and become President for Life.

PIERS (Appalled) Mff mff mff!! (Continues 'mff-ing' in the background while the others ignore him)

JULIAN WHITAKER (Growing Hitler like) Because only a strong leader can take the Parliamentary Stamp Club into the twenty-first century and meet the challenge of new currencies, shapes and adhesives! Do you know, B'Stard, the Japanese are developing an edible stamp?

ALAN I know some nouvelle cuisine restaurants in London that are already serving them. (Whitaker laughs. Alan realises Piers is still chuntering on) What do you want now, Piers? Oh, right. (Opens the door and hails passing nurse) Nurse, my friend says he feels terribly constipated and wonders if he could have a really strong enema?

PIERS	*(Protesting vehemently)* Mff! Mff mff! Mff!

ALAN	Or possibly two.

The nurse nods and goes to get the gear. Piers starts to cry.

ALAN	*(To Whitaker)* So, Jules, anything really interesting in next week's Budget?

JULIAN WHITAKER	B'Stard, I wouldn't tell you what was in my freezer, let alone the Budget!

The nurse comes in with a tray of horrific anal devices, and draws the screens around poor Piers.

JULIAN WHITAKER	*(Fastidious)* I think I ought to be toddling . . .

ALAN	Before you go . . . *(Puts hand in inside pocket and pulls out a fistful of stamps — Piers's prized stamps)* I've a few stamps here that my Uncle left me. I was going to give them to Piers to help restart his collection, but I suppose you may as well have them . . .

JULIAN WHITAKER	*(Sees they're valuable, and tries to control instant excitement)* That's very white of you . . .

ALAN	Obviously I'd want a fair price . . . *(Picking out the hundred thousand pound stamp)* Uncle Stanley always said this one was worth quite a bit . . .

JULIAN WHITAKER	*(Determined not to underestimate Alan)* Oh, yes . . . might be worth a few hundred . . . I'd have to get stuck into my Stanley Gibbons to check . . .

ALAN	Far be it from me to pry into your relationships with fellow enthusiasts . . .

JULIAN WHITAKER	No, my Stanley Gibbons stamp catalogue.

ALAN	Oh, I see . . . Look, why don't you take them, and I'll pop round to your place later this evening . . . ?

JULIAN WHITAKER	Fine, fine . . .

Suddenly there is an ear-splitting lengthy fart from behind the screens that billows the fabric.

PIERS	*(Muffled but intelligible, o.o.v.)* Bloody hell!!

ALAN   He's got his voice back, anyway.

Whitaker grins weakly and goes. Alan gets out his cellular phone and dials.

ALAN   Hello, Independent Television News? Get me Sir Alistair . . . Oh not again!? But it's only half past one! Then get me someone who can stand unaided! Hello? Who's that? Right, pay attention, John, this is one hot anonymous tip. Mmm. Ask yourself what junior Treasury minister Julian Whitaker was confiding to notorious Tory maverick Alan B'Stard, a week before the Budget? And why he's invited him to his flat this evening? Yes, pretty suspicious, don't you think?

Alan disconnects with a devious smile.

4. INT. ALAN'S HALTEMPRICE HOUSE. DAY.

Next day, early afternoon. Sarah, dressed seductively, is on the phone to Price.

SARAH   Hello, Ken? Sarah B'Stard. Yes, the lonely horseless housewife. No, Alan's in London, licking his wounds . . . and talking about licking . . .

5. INT. COMMONS BAR. DAY.

Meanwhile, Alan sits with a very large vintage cognac, watching other members going and coming. (We don't see them)

ALAN   Maggie, love the trouser suit . . . Oh, sorry Heseltine! *(Half stands)* Hey, oy, this bar is for members and accredited journalists . . . Prime Minister, didn't recognise you . . .

Alan sits, picks up newspaper to hide behind it. Then Stella Crossman, an attractive ITN journalist, about thirty, enters and sits next to him.

STELLA CROSSMAN   Alan B'Stard? *(Offers hand)* Stella Crossman, Economics Correspondent, Independent Television
News . . . I'm here because John Suchet has had a tip-off . . .

ALAN   Yes, I'd heard he was Jewish. Mind you, I hate the way
he gives himself airs and graces. Soo-shay. When I used to
know him it was pronounced Suckit. Talking of which, my
dear . . .

STELLA CROSSMAN   *(Tetchy)* Mr B'Stard, I've been warned
about your sleazy, sexist attitude. I am well briefed . . .

ALAN   I hope to catch a glimpse of them later . . .

STELLA CROSSMAN   *(Dogged)* We've had an anonymous
phone call to say you'd spent part of last night with Julian
Whitaker . . .

ALAN   What? This is outrageous! Just because I had a drink at
the home of a well-known chutney ferret . . . !

STELLA CROSSMAN   I didn't know he was . . . !? *(Alan nods)*
Then I'm even keener to know what you were doing at his flat
until two this morning, the day before Budget Day . . . ?
    *(Gets some photos out of her handbag. They show Alan sneaking
    out of a block of flats)*

ALAN   Look, if you must know, Julian was simply valuing some
old stamps I'd been left . . . Julian's very big in the Parliamentary Stamp Club.

STELLA CROSSMAN   Yes, I've read the cuttings . . .

ALAN   I was going to sell them, and use the money to build half
a dozen starter homes on a spare piece of farmland I have in
Haltemprice. Because as you probably know, the lack of
affordable accommodation for working-class villagers is a
subject close to my heart . . .

STELLA CROSSMAN   *(Disbelieving)* I find that hard to believe!

ALAN   It's true. You know, the last time I had a barbecue I had
to bus the wretched waitresses in from Leeds.

STELLA CROSSMAN   *(Disappointed)* Oh well, I suppose a
B'Stard good deed story must have some rarity value . . . we
can run it as an 'and finally . . .' When are you going to start
this building work?

ALAN   *(Bitter laugh)* When indeed? I said I *was* going to build some houses, but there's no point, not now . . . *(Stops himself)*

STELLA CROSSMAN   Not now what . . . ?

ALAN   Nothing, it doesn't matter. Where are my manners, you must let me buy you a drink . . . *(Sees back of tall, dark-haired, white-jacketed steward)* Owen! David!

The lookalike acknowledges him.

STELLA CROSSMAN   Is that who I think . . . ?!

ALAN   Yes, sad end to a great political career. We all decided to give him a fresh start as catering manager.

STELLA CROSSMAN   How extraordinary!

ALAN   No, actually he's very good, very knowledgeable on claret. One tip, though: never ask him to organise a party. Now, let's talk about us. You're a very attractive woman you know, Miss Crossman . . . Are you wearing stockings?

STELLA CROSSMAN   Why aren't you going to build the houses now? Is it something Whitaker has told you? Something to do with Tuesday's Budget?!

ALAN   No, no . . . !

STELLA CROSSMAN   Whitaker's told you something, hasn't he?! Something that affects house prices? Are they going to change the regulations on the deferment of taxation on development land . . . ?

ALAN   No, of course not!!

STELLA CROSSMAN   Then what? I won't let go, Mr B'Stard, I'm the most tenacious, ambitious journalist at ITN, and this story could make me bigger than Kate Adie!

ALAN   Big girl is she? It's hard to tell with all those shapeless clothes she wears . . .

STELLA CROSSMAN   I won't let it drop, Alan. I'll follow you around, I'll camp on your doorstep . . .

ALAN   That's all I need, another groupie! All right, Julian did let something slip out . . . and he also said something indiscreet.

STELLA CROSSMAN   What?!

ALAN   Come on, Stella, this is Professor Sex you're talking to! If I give you this hot information, I expect something hot and moist in return, and I don't mean a mutton vindaloo.

STELLA CROSSMAN You mean . . . ? *(Alan nods)* That's disgusting!

ALAN I certainly hope so. We can go back to my room, it won't take long.

STELLA CROSSMAN I know, your reputation comes before you, though word is it's the only thing that does. *(Sighs)* All right, it's a deal. You first.

ALAN Okay. *(Drops voice)* Badger Lamont's going to abolish tax relief on *(Pauses for effect)* mortgage repayments!

STELLA CROSSMAN   He is what!? But that will decimate the building industry!

ALAN   Don't tell me, one of my constituents is the biggest housebuilder in the North . . . !

STELLA CROSSMAN   This is dynamite!

ALAN   *(Gloomy)* I know . . .

STELLA CROSSMAN   . . . If it's the truth.

ALAN   Oh, that's charming! You blatantly use your sexuality to get me to betray a confidence, and then you call me a liar! *(Alan sees Whitaker enter here, as Alan knew he would, they'd arranged to meet for a drink)* Wait here. *(Crosses to Whitaker)* Jules . . . !

JULIAN WHITAKER   Alan! Have you thought about the offer I made last night?

ALAN   *(Loud enough for Stella to hear)* Yes, and I'm just not that sort of boy.

JULIAN WHITAKER   *(Looks confused)* I mean the fifty thousand for your uncle's stamps . . . ?

ALAN   I don't know, perhaps I should ask Piers for a second opinion . . .

JULIAN WHITAKER   Fletcher Dervish? What does he know about stamps? It's all he can do to find his own backside with two hands! No-one in Parliament knows more about stamps than me! Sell me those stamps, and when I'm President for Life, you can be . . . !

ALAN   Jools, not so loud! There may be Stamp Club members present. Small-minded people who might object to abolition . . .

JULIAN WHITAKER   *(Raises voice. We see Stella Crossman straining to overhear this)* I don't care who hears! Abolition is the only answer if we're to face the twenty-first century with any sort of confidence! *(Lowers voice)* Now what about my offer? I'll go up to sixty thousand. I've got the money with me . . . *(Shows him a fat wad of fifty pound notes)*

ALAN   *(Quietly)* All right, I'll bring the stamps tomorrow. *(Snatches cash)*

JULIAN WHITAKER   Excellent! *(And off he goes, gleefully)*

ALAN *(Returns to Stella)* Well, did you hear that?

STELLA CROSSMAN He's so brazen! And did I see money change hands?

ALAN Of course not! As if Julian would ask me to speculate in shares for him on the eve of the Budget!

STELLA CROSSMAN God! This will be the lead story ...! *(Rises to leave)*

ALAN But what about your promise? I thought we were going to make mad, passionate sex!?

STELLA CROSSMAN *(Looks at watch)* Sorry Alan, I can't spare the thirty seconds right now ...

ALAN Then at least promise not to mention Julian by name ...?

STELLA CROSSMAN Don't be stupid, his name makes the story!

ALAN But it'll ruin him, and he's had to work his way up from the bottom!

STELLA CROSSMAN Tough.

ALAN Then you must at least let me come on the programme and explain it was all an innocent mistake. *(Little boy act)* Please ...

6. INT. HALTEMPRICE LIVING ROOM. DAY.

A few hours later, about 5.40 pm in fact, according to the clock on the mantelpiece. A fire flickers in the grate and throws shadows on the wall. The shadows seem to show Sarah giving Ken a blow job.

KEN PRICE Yes Sarah, nearly, harder ...!

We now see that Sarah is on her knees blowing on the fire to get it to take, while Ken lies alongside her. The fire perks up and Sarah rejoins Ken on the hearth rug.

SARAH Now, where were we?

KEN PRICE We were talking about your giving me some riding lessons.

SARAH Right. Lesson one; mount the animal, grip with your knees, and try not to fall off no matter how rough the going.

KEN PRICE I think I get the hang of that . . . *(They kiss)* God, this is so great! I've got B'Stard's seat, I'm about to have his wife, and tomorrow I'm going to be worth fifty million quid . . .

Suddenly they hear Cher Titley's little voice from the hall.

CHER TITLEY *(O.O.V.)* Hello . . . ? Sarah . . . ?

KEN PRICE *(Leaps up, trousers around his ankles)* Christ, it's Cher!

SARAH I completely forgot, I invited her for tea . . .

CHER TITLEY *(Knocks and enters room)* Anyone in . . . ? *(She sees the lovers in flagrante)* Ken . . . ! Sarah!?

SARAH *(Adjusting her clothes without apparent concern)* Cher, sweetie, we're all grown-ups, all people of the world, there's no need to get upset just because your husband-to-be fancies a little mid-afternoon parallel parking with an experienced woman . . .

KEN PRICE Shut it Sarah . . . ! *(Tries to cross to Cher but is hampered by trousers at half-mast)*

SARAH After all, there are some practices Ken likes which frankly an innocent twenty-three-year-old shouldn't have to subject herself to . . .

CHER TITLEY *(Sobbing)* Ken, how could you?!

SARAH Oh, I didn't mind . . .

Cher wrenches off her big engagement ring and flings it at Ken and storms out. We hear the front door slam.

SARAH Never mind darling, she'll be back . . .

KEN PRICE *(Heart-broken)* She won't, I know her! She's proud that one . . . God, what have I done?! I must go after her!

SARAH No, that's the worst thing you can do, believe me . . . *(Tugs Ken onto the sofa and soothes him with gentle fingers)* Let her cool down, let her realise there's more to marriage than dull sexual fidelity . . . send her an expensive present tomorrow, after you become a multimillionaire. Few girls can resist a Ferrari full to the brim with caviar and diamonds . . .

KEN PRICE   But she's just thrown my engagement ring back at me! *(Shows her)*

SARAH   What, this tiddly thing? I've given bigger gems to my cleaning lady at Christmas! *(Close to Ken)* Give her some stones the size of these . . .

KEN PRICE   *(She's obviously squeezed something tender)* Ooooh . . . Yes, happen you're right . . .

SARAH   I know I am . . . *(Kisses him)* Look, let's watch the end of that video and see if Robin Hood Maid Marion with his Little John . . .

Sarah zaps on the TV, then starts looking through the pile of videos. Meanwhile the news comes on, dead on cue.

NEWSREADER   . . . Shares in building companies are expected to plummet following the leak that mortgage interest tax relief will be abolished in the Budget on Tuesday.

Ken watches, horrified.

SARAH   Here it is. *(Slips rude video in machine and turns it on. Sleazy music and grunts)*

KEN PRICE   Stupid bitch . . . !

Ken jumps forward and ejects the video. The news comes back on. On the TV screen we see Stella interviewing Alan in front of a backdrop of Westminster.

STELLA CROSSMAN   . . . And then Whitaker told you that the Chancellor intends to abolish mortgage interest at a stroke?

ALAN   Yes he did. Of course, I don't think he meant to tell me, it just sort of came out while he was making homosexual advances to me; advances which I rejected, of course.

STELLA CROSSMAN   But then did he not energetically repeat his statement in the House of Commons bar, in my presence?

ALAN   Well, yes, he did shout out something about aboli-tion . . .

Ken watches, utterly horrified.

STELLA CROSSMAN   Mr B'Stard, do you think this leak will have a damaging effect on the flotation tomorrow of Pricerite Properties, which is owned by your constituent, Kenneth Price?

ALAN   Bound to. The way I see it, there's no point offering your company to the public just when building shares are going down the toilet. If I were Ken Price, I'd postpone the whole thing, but of course he can't, because he'll already be committed to paying several million pounds worth of stockbroking commission. It's a tragedy, he's such a nice man, about to get married to a lovely girl, and this will destroy him. If you're watching Ken, I'm really sorry. *(Smirks)*

The news continues with another item. Ken stumbles out of the room, shell-shocked. Sarah smiles to herself. Then the phone rings. She answers it.

SARAH   Hello? Alan, darling ... ! Yes, we saw you on television, you were marvellous. No, I'm afraid Ken is just a teensy weensy bit put out ... So can I get on to the builders tomorrow about my indoor equestrian centre? No, of course I won't use Ken, he's far too vulgar.

Then all the lights go out. Sarah gives a little scream. Then she gropes in the drawer for something and gets out a torch and goes into the hall, rather tentatively.

SARAH   Ken ... Where are you?

Sarah comes into the hall and starts up the stairs. Then there is a shower of sparks from the ceiling. The chandelier has come adrift from its rose and is short-circuiting. The reason it has come adrift is Ken Price has hanged himself from it. Sarah's torch picks out the swinging corpse. She screams and drops the torch. Darkness.

7. INT. HOUSE OF COMMONS BAR. NIGHT.

A few days later. Alan is opening a bottle of champagne. Sarah and Piers, heavily bandaged, one arm (in 'V' shape) and one leg in plaster, are with him. Piers's jaw is now unwired.

ALAN *(To Sarah)* Well, I think everything's worked out rather well, darling.

SARAH Absolutely darling.

Alan fills three glasses and places one in Piers's plastered hand.

ALAN Well, cheers everybody.

Alan and Sarah drink. Piers can't get his glass to his lips, but in his attempt to do so he throws the drink in his own face.

SARAH You've got your seat back, I'm getting my stud . . .

ALAN And Piers will be President of the Stamp Club after all.

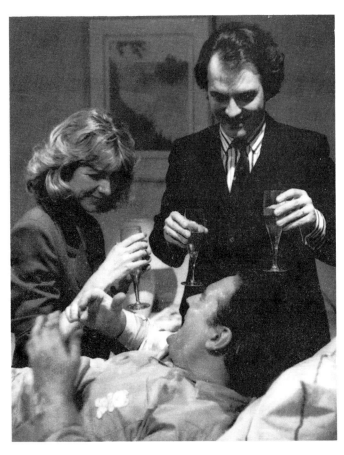

PIERS   *(Surprised)* Will I Alan?

ALAN   Of course, now Whitaker has been forced to resign.

PIERS   Oh, that's super . . . *(Looks doleful)*

SARAH   What's wrong, Piers?

PIERS   Well, all my best stamps were lost when Alan pushed me out of the train . . .

ALAN   *(Tweaks one of Piers's injuries)* When you were *blown* out of the train Piers . . .

PIERS   Ow, ow, yes, when I was blown out . . .

ALAN   Cheer up Piers; because while you were lazing around in hospital, I scoured the stamp dealers of Britain to replace your lost treasures. *(Shows Piers a new wallet containing Piers's own stamps)* Of course, they were quite expensive . . .

PIERS   *(Delighted)* Oh, I'll pay you, Alan!

ALAN   Of course you will, Piers. The invoice is in the wallet . . .

PIERS   *(Looking at stamps)* This is wonderful! You've managed to replace every single one of them. And I thought three of them were unique!

ALAN   There you go, Piers. Must be your lucky day.

Alan slaps Piers on the back. He falls to the floor and can't get up.

ALAN   Now, how are we going to celebrate, Mrs Macbeth?

SARAH   I don't know about you, darling, but I quite fancy some soft-boiled eggs. *(And off go the B'Stards, leaving Piers rocking on the floor)*

PRIME MINISTER'S OFFICE
10 DOWNING STREET SW1

B'Stard,

The Prime Minister has asked me to return the copy of your
scurrilous little book and to tell you that any repetition
of the untrue and distasteful allusion in your letter will
lead Mr Major to issue writs.

However, Mr Major is prepared to pay generously for any
information you have concerning his immediate predecessor.